C000124534

Nothing is more vital for the ch...
relevance of the whole Bible. And ...at demands fresh excitement
in simply reading it with interest and understanding. Bill Cotton
in this fascinating introduction takes the readers in one hand and
Amos in the other and walks through the rich variety and
fascinating terrain of the Old Testament. As a trustworthy and
friendly tour guide, his goal, successfully accomplished, is that
by journey's end you will feel less of a tourist and more at home
in a world which you will want to revisit often and explore in
greater depth for yourself.
Chris Wright
All Nations Christian College

Few Bible scholars have such a thorough knowledge of the Old
Testament and its background. There are even fewer who are able
to communicate it profoundly but simply by drawing relevantly
from their wealth of understanding. Bill Cotton enables the reader
to be totally immersed both in the text and also in the social,
geographical, political and religious life of Amos' day.
Derek Copley
Chairman, Evangelical Alliance

An exciting journey led by a sure-footed and experienced guide
through the life and times of the Old Testament. Using a 'zoom-
lens' technique the author begins with Amos only to set the prophet
in his wider biblical context before returning to the biblical text
which is now freshly illuminated and powerfully applied. A superb
example of how to undertake and profit from Old Testament Bible
study.
Stephen Dray
Moorlands College

A Journey through the Old Testament

with Amos as your guide

Bill Cotton

Christian Focus

I dedicate this book to my wife, Gladys, who has accompanied me in my residence in four countries, and who over 30 years has practised with me the gentle marital art of mutual encouragement.

© William Cotton
ISBN 1 85792 234 4

Published in 1995
by Christian Focus Publications,
Geanies House, Fearn, Ross-shire,
IV20 1TW, Great Britain

Printed and bound in Great Britain by
The Guernsey Press Co. Ltd., Vale, Guernsey, C.I.

Cover design by Donna Macleod

Unless otherwise stated scripture references are from the Holy Bible: New International Version copyright © 1973, 1978, 1984 by International Bible Society. Used by permission of Hodder & Stoughton Ltd., a member of the Hodder Headline Plc. Group. All rights reserved.

Contents

Preface

I wonder if Amos would be (almost) as flattered to find himself being used as a springboard into the Old Testament as I am at being asked to write a preface to Bill Cotton's deeply informed and informative study! Flattered indeed I am! During my years at Christ Church, Westbourne, I heard on many occasions and from many quarters how deeply the Old Testament Lecturer at Moorlands Bible College was immersed in his subject, how he could capture and kindle interest in every aspect of its subjects – and how many people went into Christian ministry determined to share the riches they had acquired in his classes.

I want, therefore, to send this book on its way, in the joyful expectation that what many received by word of mouth at Moorlands many thousands more will receive through the printed page. We live in a day of rising biblical illiteracy – among Christians! And if this is true about the New Testament how much more abundantly true it is of the Old! We need exactly the teaching, information, direction and encouragement this book provides in rich measure.

Amos, then, is the springboard and from now this aspect and now that of his seminal prophecy we are led, under Cotton's sure-footed guidance, to see the whole of this larger and earlier portion of God's Holy Word with enhanced understanding and appreciation. For one like me who has never been to Palestine, it has been an eye-opener to walk with Bill along the ancient highways of Israel and to see the panorama that opens out from key vantage points. But not only topography: through references culled from Amos we explore the social institutions of the Old Testament, its literature, theology, culture and religious life. The Old Testament is treated with the utmost seriousness and reverence as the very Word of God. Its problems are not shirked, above all its treasures are skilfully and amply put on display.

If you sense that I am enthusiastic about this book, you are correct.

Alec Motyer

Bishopsteignton 1997

Introduction

It is essential that you read this

Whenever the New Testament refers to 'the Scriptures' it means the books of the Old Testament, of which the Lord Jesus said ignorance would leave us in error (Matt. 22:29), which the apostle Paul said would make us wise as to salvation and would be necessary for our being built up as Christians (2 Tim. 3:16-18), and which the apostle Peter said was inspired by the prophets through the breath of the Spirit of God (2 Pet. 1:21).

This book was born on board an Italian liner. I was returning from 20 years teaching the Bible and planting churches in Bolivia and Argentina, to take up a post as lecturer in Old Testament studies at Moorlands College on the south coast of Great Britain. I reflected on the fact that my own Bible College course on 'Introduction to the Old Testament' had been frankly a bit of a bore as we skimmed through a brief analysis of every book. I remember little or nothing of the course.

Over the years in South America, teaching in various countries, I had come to see that there were two essential points which have been sadly ignored in this area. The first is that all Bible knowledge, mental and experiential, should be based on the avid reading of Scripture. Over the three years before the voyage I had engaged in a Bible reading plan, working with some eight groups of Christians, about 80 people. We had found the simple but ample reading of Scripture to be immensely refreshing to our Christian lives. I became convinced that this was a fundamental need – to *read* Scripture. Listen to it, think it through, pour our hearts into it.

The second essential point is that our Bible Study should arise out of our Bible reading. Many of us get it the other way around. We read it in small doses, meditate on it, analyse it, dissect it, etc., but the last thing we do is to actually read it – in large doses,

9

avidly. Once you do this all sorts of questions arise, and these questions become the basis of your Bible study.

If I could bring these two elements together – get my students to read the Old Testament, and then allow our study to arise out of our reading – we would achieve a very great deal. And so it has been over the past twelve years.

Of course, we could not do this by reading the whole of the Old Testament. We needed a book from it, which would be small enough to be manageable, but comprehensive enough to cover the various aspects of study which are necessary to understand its many books. We needed an essentially hands-on approach, and this we did over the years by alternating between the books of Amos and Micah. I calculate that over 500 students have worked with me through the scheme, and many have had their eyes opened to the excitement of reading, understanding and applying in our world the teaching of the various Old Testament books.

This book is not a commentary on Amos. Rather, Amos is used as a launching pad, a springboard, from which to move into a consideration of important aspects or disciplines which are essential for a comprehensive understanding of the Old Testament. The following diagram shows the various disciplines which rise out of our encounter with Amos.

FACTORS in AMOS and in all OLD TESTAMENT STUDIES

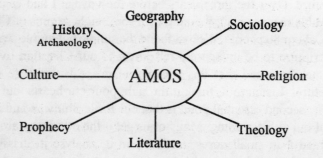

From this chart you will see that the book of Amos reflects various contributing factors. It is self-evidently prophecy, but what is the nature of prophecy? Here it is wise to ask this question of the Bible itself, rather than depend on a modern dictionary definition. Behind the prophecies of Amos lies his thought life, which we call here his theology, i.e. his ways of thinking about God. We all have theology! What he thought made him the man he was, made him do what he did, and say what he said.

But that thought has been developed at a particular point in history, within a particular country, and among particular cultural norms. So we are not surprised to find in this book history, geography and culture. You may be surprised to find sociology among our list of inquiries, but in fact the sociological realities in which Amos lived, profoundly affected his life, just as ours do today. Perhaps we shall find much in our chapter on the subject to cause us to look at our own social structures, both within our church, and beyond.

Finally the whole comes to us gift-wrapped in a certain way of writing which may seem strange to us, but which were everyday spoken forms for Amos. By comparison with other points, both inside and outside of Scripture, we can decipher the meaning of that literature.

One word of enormous consolation – at least so it has always been for me. The spiritual message of God's Word comes through though one be ignorant of the historical, geographical, cultural and other elements contained it. I would not wish that anyone should be scared into thinking that unless he/she has a grasp of the various elements contained in these chapters as important requisites for an adequate study of the Old Testament, they would be disqualified from using these biblical books for their own comfort and edification.

For example, the delightful, powerful story of David and Goliath (1 Sam. 17) has a very clear message for every one, even small children, as many a speaker among them knows. This is true regardless of whether the reader can identify the particular historic events which led up to the conflict with the Philistines, whether one can locate the valley of Elah on the map, or whether he knows that the so-called 'pebbles' of the average preacher of the story were only a little smaller than a baseball, but made of solid stone! One of these hitting the forehead at over 100 mph would mean lights out even for a giant.

This also shows how knowing these elements enriches our understanding of the Bible story, and will often provide stimulating material for the message. Incidentally, the David and Goliath story has a powerful theological content.

Each chapter of this book is complete in itself, so that it is not strictly necessary to read the book right through, though I am sure that would be the better way.

I have quoted Bible passages quite frequently, rather than require the reader to look up the biblical references, because I suspect that in the majority of cases you will find it tedious to have to look them up in order to follow the argument. So would I. However, a deeper study will always be rewarded by looking at the context. Particularly, having acquainted yourself with Amos' book, it would be useful to look back at what is being said.

I have usually quoted from the New International Version (NIV), but occasionally from the Good News Bible (GNB), when the sense of the NIV is not too clear. If I have used any other version I have indicated the source in full.

I am very grateful to my colleague Stephen Dray, who first suggested putting these studies into book form; to several friends who have read and commented on individual chapters; to Sally Jackson who has drawn the 'Gate at Dan' and the map of Israel. I am also humbled and grateful to Rev. Alec Motyer for the kind words of his Preface.

Writing is a lonely job, and I have spent many evenings working on this book. So I am grateful to my wife, Gladys, and my children, Jonathan and Mary Beth, for their patience in being so often deprived of my company.

One final word: It is essential to read the book of Amos before you begin reading this book.
Bill Cotton,
Moorlands College, Christchurch,
January, 1997

**Have you read through
the book of Amos?**

**It is absolutely essential to read the book of
Amos before you begin reading this book.
You may also find it helpful to read Amos
while following the 'Outline' on pp. 16-21.**

An Outline of the Book of Amos

G. G. Findlay described Amos as 'a man of granite, stern, fearless, self-contained, of powerful, well-knit mind, vivid imagination, and lofty bearing'. He was certainly a remarkable man, of limited social origins, yet fearless in his denunciation of evil. He appeared out of the blue on the steps of the Israelite temple at Bethel, and fiercely denounced all that was going on in the land. The Bethel temple was a royal chapel, the greatest 'cathedral' of northern Israel.

The purpose of this introductory chapter is to sketch very briefly the contents of the message of Amos, so that the reader may see that it is intelligible. Read this alongside your reading of Amos, preferably the second time.

1:1 is an introductory verse, setting the historical context in which the events of Amos' ministry occurred.

1.2 serves as the essence of the whole message of Amos, a kind of title for the book. In that case we see that his message was primarily one of the anger of the Lord against the sin of his own people, Israel.

1.3-2:8 is clearly one prophecy, with its conclusion and application in 2:9-16. Amos skilfully plays on his hearers' dislike of the neighbouring peoples – Syria, Philistia, Tyre, Edom, Ammon and Moab – by angrily attacking their militaristic designs and abuses. But these are all preparatory to an attack on his own country, Judah, followed by a longer and fiercer attack on his hearers (2:6-8). The chorus of 'amens' that will have greeted his first denunciations, will have been followed by angry scowls as he pitched into the abuses of the Israelites, which had been perpetrated, not against other nations, but against their own people and institutions.

2:9-16 applies the consequences of these evils to his hearers. First, in typical prophetic fashion, he spells out the great love and kindness that the Lord has shown toward the Israelites (9-12); then he attacks the way they have trampled on their privileges. Judgment is imminent and will be inescapable (13-16).

3:1-2 the opening words of this chapter, *'Hear this word...'*, indicate a second prophecy which will cover two chapters. Verse 2 represents the theme of the message of the whole book. The Lord has entered into intimate relationship with Judah/Israel. The prophet clearly considers Israel and Judah to be one family and for that very reason her privileges will lead to dire punishment for disobedience.

3:3-8 These verses constitute Amos' explanation of the motivating springs of his ministry. They answer the question, 'What authority does this upstart have to come and preach at us in this way?' His answer is based on a cause and effect logic. You see or hear certain things, and you know that behind these events there is an explanation. In this case, what you see is a man preaching. What is the explanation, the cause that lies behind the happening? Answer: *'The Sovereign LORD has spoken – who can but prophesy?'* It is Amos' unerring conviction that God has admitted him to his audience chamber, and has revealed his 'plan' to him.

3:9-15 Once more, punishment is coming. The evil rampant in Israel is an international scandal (v. 9); violence and robbery prevail (v. 10); so destruction is about to come, its chief objective being to destroy the idolatry and luxury of those who hold the reigns of power.

4:1-3 Behind the men who exploit their fellow men, are found wives who have an insatiable appetite for more luxurious ways of living. They will be among the first to go out to misery and slavery.

4:4-5 A satirical call to worship. Bethel and Gilgal were important historical places in Israel, but they had become adulterated by evil practices.

4:6-13 Because of this evil the Lord has sent a series of minor judgments: famine, drought, blighted crops, plagues, warfare and destruction. These were sent to awaken the consciences of the Israelites, but they have largely failed. So they should now prepare to meet their God in the fires of destruction (v. 12). Verse 13 is a poetical affirmation of the universal power of the Lord, whereby he is able to carry out his threats to the full.

5:1-17 This is a third prophecy. It is set in the form of a 'lament' (v. 1). A lament is the term in the Old Testament for a funeral dirge. Probably the prophet dressed appropriately for the occasion in sackcloth and sprinkled his head with ashes. He tolls the death-knell for the funeral of Israel (v. 2). Yet, like all the prophets, Amos is convinced that all is not lost, and that the slightest sign of true repentance will lead to the reviving of the corpse (vv. 4-6).

Verses 7-15 spell out the way in which justice and righteousness have been trampled into the ground (v. 7), as the poor have been cruelly exploited, and the judicial system corrupted in favour of the rich. The conclusion of the offer of repentance is, *'Hate evil, love good; maintain justice in the courts. Perhaps the LORD God Almighty will have mercy on the remnant of Joseph'* (v. 15).

It would seem, however, that Amos is convinced that the invitation will not be heeded, and so the funeral cortege proceeds to its final destiny (vv. 16-17).

5:18-27 The prophet turns on the false confidences in religion harboured by the people, which lead to the fixation that the Lord will never punish them. First, 18-20, is the privileged position they hold, whereby the coming Day of the Lord will result in Israel's salvation and the punishment of all their enemies. Not so, says Amos. In that day all sinners will be punished, regardless of any privileged position.

The second false confidence was in their religious activities. It was not that the people didn't go to 'church', or didn't practice their religion. On the contrary they had a supreme confidence that their religious acts made them acceptable to God. Amos tears this rag of confidence apart and declares that the Lord hates and despises their religious acts. They will not avert the anger of God. There is only one remedy: *Let justice roll on like a river, righteousness like a never-failing stream!* (v. 24).

6:1-7 He now turns on the country's rulers, giving a graphic picture of their luxury life-style, and assuring them that they will be the first to go into exile (v. 7).

6:8-14 Once more Amos concludes his sermon with the certainty of divine judgment on the nation. The reason for divine judgment is again spelt out in terms of injustice: *You have turned justice into poison and the fruit of righteousness into bitterness* (v. 12).

By now you may have got weary of the theme of divine judgment. Don't worry, you are in good company. So did his hearers!

Chapter 7 We now have a complete change of tempo. Whilst almost everything to this point has been set in poetic form, note the short lines, much of this chapter is in prose. It provides the physical background to everything else in the book.

7:1-9 In these verses Amos relates three visions. These were what led to his presence in Bethel. All three visions have to do with divine judgment. In the first two Amos intercedes, and the Lord suspends the judgment. It is probable that they came over a period of time, with an interval between each. In the third vision, however, Amos knows that the days of prayer for Israel have passed, that inevitably divine judgment must fall. Yet he sped up north to warn Israel, in the hope that repentance produced through his message would bring salvation.

7:10-17 It was not to be. So far from repenting, there was an almost violent confrontation with Amaziah, the chief priest at Bethel. Amaziah sent word to the king accusing Amos of seeking to subvert the nation, and whilst he waited for reinforcements, he confronted him and told him to get back to Judah. So far from being intimidated, Amos' reaction is to reaffirm his divine calling, and to assure the priest that destruction would most certainly come, and would affect his whole family.

Chapters 8 and 9:1-10 contain the last message of Amos, perhaps preached even as he packed his bags. It is based on two further visions.

8:1-3 In the first vision he sees a basket of ripe fruit. The nation is ripe for destruction, *I will spare them no longer.*

8:4-6 Once again he shows anger against those who exploit the common people, in this case the merchants *who trample the needy* in order to enrich themselves.

8:7-14 The Lord has seen this exploitation, and his condemnation is sure and severe: *I will never forget anything they have done.* Terrible destruction is coming upon them, which will wipe away their joy, and make them a nation marked by mourning, weeping, and bitterness.

9:1-4 The 5th vision reminds us of the Samson story. However, in this case it is the Lord who plays the Samson role, as he destroys the pillars of the temple, obviously of Bethel, and the whole lot comes crashing down. It might be that some will escape this and seek to flee far away from the wrath of God, but this will be to no avail as he will follow and destroy them wherever they go.

9:5-6 This is one of three tributes of praise to the Lord Almighty, which at times seem to interrupt the flow of the text. If they are seen as affirmations of the divine power of the Lord, the God of Israel, they are intelligible. The God of Israel is no petty, local, national god, he is the Lord of the universe, who is able to perform all he warns he will do.

9:7-10 Isaiah named his first-born Shear-Jashub, a most strange-sounding name, but which was full of portent. It meant 'a remnant shall return'. This is at one and the same time a threat and a promise. The threat – destruction and exile is certain; the promise – the nation would not be obliterated, a remnant would be conserved. These last verses of Amos' message say the same thing. As a kingdom the nation would be *destroyed from the face of the earth – yet I will not totally destroy the house of Jacob* (v. 8).

9:11-15 This last passage of the book seems to some to sit unevenly with the contents of the rest of the book. It is full of a glorious hope for the eventual restoration of the nation. I think it probable that Amos never preached this as a message. Perhaps he appended it when the book was completed. It certainly sits well with the previous verses in which God has promised that he will not completely destroy the nation.

I trust that this brief outline will have given you an idea of the flow of the thought of Amos, and that it will encourage you to read it again. Some questions will have been raised in your mind, and I hope that they will find answers in the text of the book.

A Christian lady told me that she did not like Amos: 'He is too stern. I like something from the Word of God that is comforting.' If we believe that the Bible is the inspired Word of God, we are duty bound to listen to all its parts, and we have no right to be selective. It is especially dangerous to major only on those parts which make us feel comfortable. God's Word has many uncomfortable things to say to us, in order to challenge us, not so much to achieve the good, as to achieve the best.

ROADS:
① The Way of the Sea.
② The King's Highway.
③ Highway from Jezreel Valley to Beersheba.
④ Road from Joppa to Jericho and beyond.

1

Amos' Place in History

The first chapter of Amos is appalling. We read:

the Syrians *treated the people of Gilead with savage cruelty;*

the Philistines *carried off a whole nation and sold them as slaves to the people of Edom;*

Tyre *carried off a whole nation into exile in the land of Edom, and did not keep the treaty of friendship they had made;*

the Edomites *hunted down their brothers, the Israelites, and showed them no mercy; Their anger had no limits, and they never let it die;*

In their wars for more territory, the Ammonites *even ripped open pregnant women;*

the Moabites *dishonoured the bones of the king of Edom by burning them to ashes* (from Amos 1:3-2:3, all quotes from GNB).

A good case for anyone concerned with human rights and the Geneva Convention! Here is a shepherd who is concerned about crimes practised in the community of nations, as also among his own people. Quite clearly these are descriptions of real events, and they come in a series of condemnations which the prophet makes against those peoples which surrounded the land of Israel – Syrians, Philistines, Tyrians, Moabites, Ammonites, Edomites – strange names to us, but real people to Amos.

Whatever one might think of such shocking statements, one can hardly say that they are 'boring', which is the attitude many of us have toward the reading of history. Amos is not a history book, but one can detect historic events in many parts. This is important because God's revelation of himself is rooted in history.

Before the Earthquake, 760 BC

History appears in the first verse of Amos. His message was pronounced *two years before the earthquake*. This is very precise. Presumably the earthquake needed no word of explanation to the readers. It is probable that his words at 9:5 – *The sovereign LORD Almighty touches the earth and it quakes; all who live in it mourn* (GNB) – were seen as a prophecy of this event, and that when it happened people knew that his words were fulfilled. Can we give a date to this earthquake? It would seem that this is the earthquake referred to 240 years later by Zechariah: *You will flee as you fled from the earthquake in the days of Uzziah* (14:5). It was such a shattering earthquake that it was still being talked about 200 years later! Excavators at Hazor in northern Israel found evidence of an earthquake, which they dated to 760 BC, which fits admirably with the times of Uzziah and of Amos.

So the very first verse lands us in a specific historic situation. Indeed it is probable that they limit the time of Amos' prophecy to one, perhaps two years before the earthquake. This need not surprise us, since Haggai's recorded prophecy lasted only four months (cf. Haggai 1:1; 2:1,10 and 20), and it is probable that Amaziah, the self-serving, power-serving, arrogant priest of Bethel will have had the political clout to have Amos expelled from the country – *Get out you seer! Go back to the land of Judah* (7:12).

Looking back – The Division of the Kingdom

We learn something further from verse one. Amos preached during the reigns of Uzziah, king of Judah, and Jeroboam, king of Israel. Now this seems rather confusing. The casual reader may have some idea of 'Israel' as one people, one nation. Sadly, at a particular juncture in their history the unity of the nation was split apart by internal strife.

The story is given in detail in 1 Kings 12. During the latter part of his reign Solomon had imposed forced labour, heavy taxes, and severe oppression on his own people to pay for his ambitious state projects. This led to much bitterness and anger among the ten northern tribes, who split from the south. The one nation became two. A confrontation at Shechem was an attempt to heal the breach, but only widened it and led to a division into two kingdoms, which was never to be healed.

Relationships between Israel and Judah were often strained. We must be careful, however, not to view these relationships in terms of the modern nation-state. The situation was much more fluid. There were no clearly defined borders between the two countries, no border controls, and since people of the two nations had kinship relationships, coming and going was fairly easy.

The most important thing to notice is that during the reign of Uzziah and Jeroboam the two 'nations' were passing through a period of maximum growth, militarily, economically, and physically in terms of territorial expansion. With the old world powers passing through a period of great weakness things had never been so good for Israel/Judah since the Empire days of David and Solomon. Power and expansion brought wealth, but what both Amos, and Hosea his northern contemporary, show is that this wealth was accumulated in the hands of a few and led to the exploitation of the poor, gross immorality and idolatry. Amos gives us a sad picture of the powerful and wealthy people milking Israel's good fortunes for themselves, principally by exploiting the poor for all they were worth.

Hosea shows that worship of the false god, Baal, had returned like a flood (Hos. 2). It is probable Jeroboam had improved relations with Tyre, the heartland of the worship of Baal.

We must picture Amos, a southerner, visiting the north quite frequently, perhaps to sell wool. He saw the idolatry, immorality and exploitation that was going on. His heart burned with anger. We do well to ask ourselves whether we burn with indignation when seeing evil.

Jeroboam II and Uzziah, the two kings mentioned by Amos, both had very long reigns and no frictions with each other. His obituary notice said of Jeroboam: *He restored the boundaries of*

Israel from Lebo Hamath to the Sea of the Arabah, i.e. from a
sizable portion of Syrian territory, through that of Ammonites,
Moabites and Edomites, east of the Jordan River. In the south
Uzziah subdued the Philistines and Arabian tribes, so that *his fame
spread as far as the borders of Egypt, because he had become
very powerful* (2 Chron. 26:8).

Looking further back – the Exodus from Egypt

Amos casts his mind back to the central historic fact of the Old
Testament, the liberation of Israel from Egyptian slavery at the
Exodus. This was the most important single fact in the collective
memory of the people of Israel, being written into their laws, their
feasts, their Temple songs, and their poetry. Amos, like many
other prophets, uses the Exodus to remind Israel of the Lord's
kindness to her, and of her base ingratitude (2:10).

At 3:1,2 he uses the Exodus theme to emphasize both the
oneness of the people of Israel – *the whole family I brought up
out of Egypt* – and the divine election, whereby Israel became the
people of the Covenant. See also 4:10. Yet Amos will not allow
the people to gloat over their favoured position, for historically
the Lord also brought up *the Philistines from Caphtor* (Crete)
and the Aramaeans (Syrians) *from Kir* (9:7). He is God over all
the nations.

Amos plays on the Exodus theme. During the night of the flight
from Egypt the Lord had passed over the people of Israel as the
avenging angel passed through the midst of the Egyptians. From
this point throughout biblical history, and even today, the Jews
have celebrated annually the Passover. However, Amos hears the
Lord affirm twice, '*I will not again* pass by *them any more*' (7:8
and 8:2), on both occasions spelling out the rejection of Israel. In
5:16-17 he pictures Israel as a funeral procession, and concludes,
'*I will* pass through *your midst*', as he did to the Egyptians. Not
only so, but the grief they will experience will be *like mourning
for an only son* (8:10), a threat intended to remind them of the

death of the first-born in Egypt when the angel of God's wrath swept over that country at the Exodus. From Amos' view they had become so corrupt, they merited the same disaster as had been experienced by Egypt.

Amos' knowledge of history, geography, and current events

One of the most remarkable facts is that Amos, a sheep farmer, should have had such an extensive knowledge of the world around him, both its history and recent developments. Here is a lesson for us. We are not expected by God to be social recluses, buried in our local churches, ignorant of the world around us. It was only as Amos concerned himself for both the past and the present of his people that he had a message for them. God's guidance does not work in a mental and social vacuum.

Amos' message is thus rooted in history. In the same way the coming of Jesus, his earthly life in an artisan's cottage, his public teaching, his death and resurrection are rooted in history. He was born in a particular place and time: Bethlehem in the reign of King Herod the Great; was educated in a specific place and time: Nazareth; was crucified in Jerusalem City during the governorship of the Roman, Pontius Pilate. These are historic facts and they serve as the heart of our Christian faith.

We are now in a position to move beyond the history of Amos' days to a wider perspective of Old Testament history.

A Potted Overview of Old Testament History

Biblical References

Time Line BC

Amos can be safely dated around the year 760 BC, but Israel's history dates back 1300 years before his time. The time line is given in the right column and you will see this reducing as BC history does till the birth of Jesus.

The Patriarchs, Egypt and the Exodus.

Genesis 12-14

Abraham was a wanderer, a semi-nomad, who lived on the edge of the desert or among the towns slightly inland from the desert.

±2000

Genesis
25-27

He was followed by his son, Isaac, who was born after years of agonised prayer and longing. To Isaac was born Jacob who is pictured in Genesis as the father of the twelve tribes of Israel, outstanding among whom was his son Joseph.

37-50

Joseph's story occupies a large part of Genesis. He was sold into slavery by his brothers, but through a remarkable series of divine leadings he emerged as the highest official in Egypt, second only to the Pharaoh. His wit and wisdom, inspired by his God, lead Egypt into plentiful resources when the rest of the world is devastated by drought. All roads lead to Egypt, and eventually his brothers appear there. After a series of manipulations, whereby Joseph searches the hearts of his brothers to see whether they are the same evil, cynical men as before, he reveals himself to them and gives them a place in Egypt.

±1760

Exodus
1:8

After Joseph's death, *a new king, who did not know about Joseph, came to power in Egypt.* Frightened by the growth of the minority group of Israelites in his country, he embarked on a policy of repression, subjecting them to forced labour on important building projects. It is often surmised that this Pharaoh was Ramesses II, renowned for his colossal building programme. Some would place the date much earlier, about 1440. Since Scripture does not give us his name, we must hold any theory tentatively. From a biblical point of view it is of little importance.

±1650

1280

(1440)

The Book of Exodus tells us that in the midst of this misery, and confronting a new policy of genocide, God raised up a deliverer in the person of Moses. There were various confrontations between Moses and the Pharaoh, but after a series of remarkable miracles, each of which brought misery to the Egyptians, the Pharaoh begged the Israelites to leave, which they did with alacrity. In spite of a change of mind on his part, followed by the destruction of his armies in the Red Sea, the Israelites made good their escape.

Exodus 1-2

Exodus 7-11

But freedom from Egyptian slavery was not designed to give them the liberty to be their own bosses, to decide their own future. In the desert they pitched tents at Mt. Sinai and there received the Law of the Lord through the mediation of Moses. This, composed of the Ten Commandments of Exodus 20 and the various social stipulations of Exodus 21-23, formed the basis of a unique relationship between God and Israel, who now revealed himself to them with the covenant name of 'Yahweh'.

Exodus 20-24

The Exodus (literally, 'the Way Out' = the flight from Egypt), the Law, the Covenant, Election and Promise become fundamental ideas by which the people of Israel bound themselves in willing service to Yahweh their God. For hundreds of years after this, these realities will be inscribed in the very heart of everything Israel does in her finer moments. We find Amos, along with all the other prophets, using them as the yardstick by which

Exodus 24:3-8

to measure the people's faithfulness to the Lord.

The Wilderness Wanderings and the Occupation of Canaan

Exodus 32

Even so, Israel found it hard to be faithful to God. At Sinai itself she fell into faithlessness and idolatry. Later her nerve failed her when confronted with the might of the Canaanites, with the consequence that she was condemned to wander for 40 years in the wilderness.

1240 (1400)

Numbers 13-14

Eventually she did arrive at Canaan, but through the back door – Jericho, and by a series of lightning attacks to the centre, south and north of the land. Under Joshua's leadership she effectively crippled many of the major cities of the native inhabitants. However, the book of Judges makes clear that it took her some time to make good her possession of the land, the most decisive battle being that against the King of Hazor, under Deborah and Barak.

Joshua 1-10

Judges 4-5

Even so, it was not until the time of their own king, David, that the Israelites were able finally to choke off all opposition and achieve total control of the land. This was at least 250 years after their initial destruction of Jericho. During these years Israel was governed sporadically by a series of dynamic leaders, whom the Lord raised up at critical periods of their history. Such periods were not simply the natural consequence of events beyond their control, but followed a regular cycle of apostasy by the Israelites as they hankered after the gods of

1000

the native population, the rain god Baal and Asherah his consort.

Canaanite religion was essentially sexual in character. Since fertility was the fundamental need of primitive peoples – fertility of the land, of the herd and flock, of the human body – sex came to hold a central place in their worship. Within their temples they practised imitative magic. If man copulates on earth, the gods see it and are stirred to copulate in the heavens, with the result that rain comes and fertility is guaranteed to man. So prostitutes provided sexual indulgence within the temples. A society – and this was not the actions of a fringe sect but an indulgence of the whole people – reared on such sensual excitement could not get enough entertainment, so child sacrifice also became part of the worship.

The Israelites successively found this religion both repulsive and fascinating. The local people, whom they had permitted to remain in the land against the will of the Lord, will have assured them that this was the way to get results from the gods, and so great numbers of the Israelites indulged in Baalism.

The Lord was angry with these evil acts and gave them over to their enemies, who cruelly repressed them, until they cried out to him in their distress. Again and again he was moved to pity, raised up a deliverer, and saved them from their enemies. For a time, whilst the deliverer, or 'judge', lived they obeyed the

Lord, but as soon as he was removed from the scene they promptly slipped back into apostasy, and the cycle began again, with continually deteriorating effects.

In spite of some important victories over other neighbours, the Philistines, who had settled in the south-west corner of the land, proved too powerful for God's people. This period is the beginning of the Iron Age, when iron became the decisive military factor. The Israelites were ignorant of iron working and *I Samuel* were obliged to go cap in hand to the *13:20* Philistines even to get their sickles sharpened.

I Samuel It was the Philistine menace, culminating in a *8:5* humiliating defeat at Aphek in the year 1050, which eventually led to the demand for *a king to lead us, like all the other nations have.* Historically it has always been so. In a loosely federated state the greatest demand for strong central government has risen from the need for a stronger defence system against common enemies. So it was in Israel.

1050

Samuel warned that the solution of short term needs would result in tragic long-term consequences, as we shall see when we look at the sociology of Amos in chapter 6.

The Monarchy – Kings Saul, David and Solomon

The nation then lived under these three kings for 120 years. Saul, though valiant in his early years, turns out to be a depressive, who

1050-930

distrusts everybody, especially those nearest and dearest to him. The performance of the young David in confronting the giant Goliath, and thus throwing the Philistines into dismay and rout, becomes a threat to Saul's kingship, particularly to his dynastic succession. He spends many years hunting down David, who becomes a fugitive from the fury of Saul, ever on the move, bringing together a band of ruffians, hiding in caves and hills.

I Samuel 17

I Samuel 18-27

Saul's greatest problem, however, was not with his own temperament, nor yet with David, but with his inability to deal with the Philistine menace, and eventually he died in battle on Mt. Gilboa, to the south-east of the Jezreel Valley.

I Samuel 28-30

For a time there was civil war. Saul's son Ish-Bosheth claimed the throne, whilst David staked his claim on having been chosen by the Lord rather than by any dynastic right. He reigned for seven years at Hebron in the south, until finally Ish-Bosheth's supporters betrayed and murdered him, and switched their allegiance to David.

2 Samuel 3-4

David was an astute king. Having finally crushed the Philistines, he quickly moved against the Jebusite stronghold in Jerusalem, establishing it as his new capital, located no longer in Judah, but just over the border in Benjamite territory. From here he moved out in a series of military combats, till he had absorbed various other small states around.

2 Samuel 5

2 Samuel ch. 8

996

This was a time of power vacuum in the Near East as the great powers were in eclipse, and David was able to establish a sizable empire.

David's son Solomon was the first dyn-   970-930
astic leader of Israel. All other leaders had been chosen by the Lord and displayed more than natural gifts, which were seen by the biblical historians as showing the enveloping power of the Spirit of God upon them. Solomon's kingship was of a radically different type, i.e. dynastic. He established friendly relationships with the
I Kings   Egyptians by marrying the Pharaoh's
3   daughter, and with the great commercial port of Tyre by good trade relations.

He built the temple in Jerusalem and inaugurated worship therein. Since Israel
I Kings   lay astride the great trunk road from
5-9   Mesopotamia to Egypt he was able to exploit the business opportunities of his position. He carefully built up and fort- ified three cities, Hazor, Megiddo and Gezer, which lay along this road within Israelite territory. He imported spices from Saba, modern Yemen. His court became famous as the centre of much
I Kings   learning, with important visitors coming
4:29-34   to him from various parts of the world.

However, pride got the better of him. He
I Kings   began to reorganize the districts of the
10   country along different lines than those

of the old tribal areas, imposing heavy taxes
to support his luxurious court and building
works. The corvée system, whereby Israelites
were required to give one in three months to
the State for unpaid labour, caused great anger
among his subjects, especially those outside
his own tribe of Judah.

The Division of Israel and Judah

The policies of Solomon finally drove the
northern tribes, under the leadership of the
tribe of Ephraim, to revolt. Rehoboam, Solomon's son, went to Shechem in the heart of
the northern territory, probably as a con-
ciliatory gesture, to be crowned king. Here the
northern tribes demanded retraction of all
Solomon's oppressive laws, but after consultation with the young men with whom he
had gone to school, he threatened an even more
oppressive regime. This inevitably led to the
breaking up of the kingdom, as the northern
tribes established their own country, calling
themselves Israel, leaving the southern tribe
to its own name, Judah.

Rehoboam's first instinct was to impose his
law, but when his tax-collector arrived in the
north he was stoned to death. He called out
his army, and was about to go to war, when a
prophet warned him against such a venture,
since this was the Lord's doing. He became
an evil king, even permitting 'male-shrine
prostitutes' to proliferate in Judah. For his sins
he was attacked by Pharaoh Shishak, and the
temple was pilfered of all its gold, which surely

Margin references:

I Kings 11-12

I Kings 12

I Kings 14:25-28

Margin dates:

930

925

raises the question of the wisdom of Solomon
in building such costly edifices adorned with
gold and silver.

I Kings
12:25-33

Jeroboam I became king of the north, his capital
in Shechem. His immediate problem was the
danger, so he supposed, of the people
continuing to make the three annual treks to
Jerusalem, so he set up counter religious centres
at Bethel and Dan. It was at one of these, Bethel,
that our friend Amos preached. On various
occasions, recording the accession of a new
king, the biblical historian comments, *he clung
to the sins of Jeroboam.... which he had caused
Israel to commit.*

2
Chroni-
cles
14:8-15

Over the next 200 years these two petty states
led a chequered existence. Judah was the most   930-972
stable, and some of her kings were to be
commended as men who sought to do the will
of God. Among those especially applauded are
Asa, Jehoshaphat, Joash and Uzziah (also
called Azariah). Yet even these showed by their
tendency to pride and occasional lusts for
power, the deficiencies in the system of
kingship. Thus Asa, whilst praying humbly for

2
Chroni-
cles 16

God's strength against the Ethiopians and
experiencing a remarkable victory, lost his
nerves when later confronted by the threat of   900
Israel, and appealed to Syria to attack the northern country, for which lack of faith he was
sternly rebuked by a prophet. So far from hum-   875
bling himself, he unleashed a reign of terror to
silence all criticism. He may have been a good
'king' but he was certainly no democrat.

The north, Israel, on the other hand, does not have even one king to be commended, and whilst the Davidic dynasty in Judah maintained its existence for 21 kings and 340 years, the north's existence was punctuated by constant internal strife, assassinations, and civil war. At one point there were four kings – Elah, Zimri, Omri/Tibni – in the course of one week! Strong leaders emerged in the persons of Omri and his son Ahab. Omri moved the capital to the impregnable Samaria, and astutely married off Ahab to a princess of the royal family of Sidon, closely linked to Tyre, the leading commercial nation of the world, but also a centre of Baal worship. Jezebel by name, she was determined that the worship of Baal should become the accepted form of worship in her husband's land.

I Kings 16:9-21

I Kings 16:24

876

It was this that led to the famous confrontation of Elijah and Ahab on Mt. Carmel, which, incidentally was significant as being both the frontier and disputed territory between the Baal people and Israel. Not that Jezebel wanted to wipe out the old religion, since her children all bore names with either endings in -iah (= a shortened form of Yahweh, the God of Israel), Ahaziah and Athaliah, or with Jeh- beginnings, which again signifies Yahweh. What she wanted was equal rights for her own people's religion, and that meant full state recognition. This would eventually have meant the end of the worship of Yahweh.

I Kings 18

860

2
Chroni-
cles
20:35-37

850

At this time relations between the northern and southern kingdoms, Israel and Judah, reached a harmonious level. Jehoshaphat made league with Israel by marrying Ahab's daughter, Athaliah, daughter also, let it be remembered, of Jezebel. Athaliah had all the passion for Baalism that her mother had. She was now queen in Jerusalem.

The Year of Horrendous Massacres, 842. If a century later Amos had reason to berate the neighbouring peoples for their cruelty, the bloodbath perpetrated in both Israel and Judah at this point makes their cruelty seem mild. Elijah was not the only opponent of Baal worship. A military commander called Jehu, busily defending the city of Ramoth-Gilead against the Syrians, was called upon by Elisha to destroy the remnants of Baalism.

842

2 Kings 9

He did this with great zeal. He first killed Joram, the reigning king of Israel, and Jezebel the queen mother in Jezreel. By chance Ahaziah, the king of Judah, was visiting that city, so Jehu dispatched him as well. He then had the heads of 70 princes of Ahab's household hacked off and delivered to him in baskets! Anyone with any connections with the old regime was slaughtered without mercy. He then posed as a worshipper of Baal, called the god's worshippers together in their 'cathedral' in the capital, Samaria, had the doors sealed and let in his soldiers to hack the people to death.

I Kings
10

I Kings
11

Athaliah, now Queen Mother in Jerusalem, heard with horror of the murder of her son, and of the destruction of all that her mother, Jezebel, represented. She promptly went into overdrive, having all the royal princes of Jerusalem killed, and installing herself as queen. However, a baby was spirited away and hidden in the temple, being proclaimed king at six years by the priests. This led to Athaliah's death. Think of this, but for this slender thread, this 6-year-old boy, the Messianic line of David would have been wiped out. This was surely a Satanic ploy, but God's plans for Jerusalem and the Messiah Christ could never be destroyed.

837

Hosea
1:4

100 years later the Lord, through the prophet Hosea roundly condemned the bloodbath of 742: 'Call him (your baby son) Jezreel, because I will soon punish the house of Jehu for the massacre at Jezreel, and I will put an end to the kingdom of Israel.'

750

The Assyrian Fox in Israel's Hen Shed. The bloodiness of Jehu greatly weakened the northern nation for seventy years. The 2,000 chariots which King Ahab had fielded against Assyria in 853, according to Assyrian records, were reduced to only 10. In spite of a resurgence under Jeroboam II, Israel could not stand for long, and he was followed by 20 years of anarchy, in which time six kings came in rapid succession, only one of whom died naturally. These were the times of our friend Amos. He saw the writing on the wall, yet whilst he saw a foreign nation about to destroy this people, he did not name the aggressor.

786-746

2 Kings
13:7

760

15 years later Tiglath-Pileser III, often called
Pul, came to the Assyrian throne and began the
march of world empire. Kings of the land of   745
the god Ashur (from which Ashuria=Assyria)
were expected to expand their empire by military might. Pul developed a mighty war-
machine, such as the world till that time had
never seen, and Assyria was on the move. Museums containing artifacts of the ancient world
give chilling testimony to the hideous cruelty
in which the empire revelled.

Petty states like Israel and Judah had to decide
where their loyalties lay, and design their
political decisions accordingly. The northern
kingdom decided to resist, and joined Syria in
an alliance to this end. However, having Judah
at their backs could have been very dangerous,
so Israel and Syria marched against Jerusalem.

2 Kings
16:5-9
Panic seized Judah, but the prophet Isaiah
exhorted King Ahaz of Jerusalem to stand firm

Isaiah
7:1-9
in his faith, and to trust in Yahweh. Ahaz did
not rise to the occasion and implored the   734
Assyrian king to come to his aid, thus inviting
the fox into the hen house. Pul was delighted
by the invitation and lost no time in destroying
Damascus, capital of Syria. He attacked Israel,
and deported the population of Galilee and
Trans-Jordan, decimating the land of Israel with
its capital in Samaria, reducing it to 1/3 of its
former size. This was certainly not what Ahaz
had intended.

The price of Assyria's help for Judah was a
protection racket. Ahaz was required to place

the altar of the Assyrian god in the centre of
temple worship in Jerusalem, which he did with
alacrity. The worship of Yahweh was pushed
to one side, and a yearly tribute was paid to the
Assyrians.

2 Kings
16:10-18

Samaria also paid tribute, but eventually re-
belled, expecting help from Egypt. This failed   725
and Shalmaneser V of Assyria laid siege to
Samaria. So powerful was this city, built by
Omri and Ahab, that it took the Assyrians three
years to bring about its surrender. By then
Sargon was king of Assyria – he claims to have
taken more than 27,000 captives, deporting   722
them to distant lands. *This was the end of the
northern kingdom*, and Amos had played his
part in prophesying such an outcome (Amos
9:1-10). Israel was scattered in three provinces
of Assyria and other peoples were put into the
vacuum of Samaria. These became the Samaritans of whom we read in the New Testament.

2 Kings
17

17:24-3

Following the death of Ahaz of Judah, the
young king Hezekiah, profoundly influenced   715
by Isaiah, rebelled against Assyria. It took some
years for a new king of Assyria, Sennacherib,
to finally get around to dealing with Judah, but   701
in 701 his armies swept in, devastating 46
towns and villages, taking over 200,000
captives away to Assyria. Only one city was
left standing in Judah – Jerusalem, *like a hut
in a field of melons*. However, the siege of that
city was lifted by the decimation of the
Assyrian army in a terrible plague. Sennacherib
was forced to return home. This event is

2 Kings
18-19

Isaiah
1:8

recorded in full detail three times in the Old Testament.

Sadly, what had been a demonstration of Yahweh's saving grace, became the root of a false doctrine in Jerusalem – the impregnability of the city. People reasoned that since the city had defied the might of the Assyrian army and won, it could never be defeated. This was bolstered by the argument that this was the city of the Lord, that his temple was located in it, and that the elect Davidic dynasty reigned within it. Even the priest-prophet Ezekiel required a special revelation, in which he saw the Glory of God moving out of the temple and away from the city, before he was convinced that it could and would fall.

Ezekiel 10

In spite of Sennacherib's devastation and siege, Judah and Jerusalem were to continue for more than 100 years. For 80 years of these Assyria continued as the dominant world power, rising to its zenith under Ashurbanipal, during whose time the evil king Manasseh ruled Judah for something like 50 years. He crushed all opposition, stifled prophecy, introduced Assyrian star and sun worship, and *shed so much innocent blood that he filled Jerusalem from end to end.* He suppressed all opposition by a reign of terror.

700-586

2 Kings 21

2 Kings 21:16

Nebuchadnezzar and Babylon

In 612 the combined forces of Media and Babylon attacked Nineveh, capital of the Assyrian Empire, and destroyed it. For another

612

eight years remnants of the Empire clung on, but finally their last stronghold in Carchemish fell. From here Nebuchadnezzar turned his attention to the south – Tyre, the Philistine cities, and Judah, all en route to his ultimate goal, conquest of Egypt.

2 Kings 23:29-30

608

Josiah, king of Judah, a godly king who sought to reform the faith and morals of his kingdom, had foolishly sought to oppose Pharaoh Neco's attempt to go to the aid of the Assyrians, and was killed at Megiddo. With his death the country reverted overnight to idolatry, immorality and exploitation.

2 Kings 24

607

Josiah was followed by four mediocre or evil kings (three of them were his own sons). They were constantly warned by the prophet Jeremiah of the dire consequence of disobedience to the Lord, but none would listen. Jeremiah himself was put on trial on a charge of treason because he warned solemnly of the coming disaster and exhorted the people of Jerusalem to surrender to the Babylonians and go quietly into exile.

2 Kings 25

586

Eventually, the stubborn resistance of the people resulted in the Babylonian attack on the city, its fall, and the depopulation of the whole country. Many thousands were deported, 1,300 kilometres (800 miles) to distant Babylon, there to begin a new life, far away from the land they loved. To many it seemed that this was the end for Israel. Their capital, Jerusalem, now lay in complete ruin. They had believed it to be the

centre of the world, Yahweh's throne. It now
appeared like an insignificant provincial town
in comparison with the glory of the mighty
city of Babylon, to which they were deported.

Creeping doubt could have paralysed the
nation. There were those who doubted the
Lord's power, his ability to save Israel; there
were those who doubted his justice, believing
that they did not deserve to be expelled from
their land; there were those, the more godly,
who doubted his grace. Had he abandoned
Israel forever? The Lord's reply was decisive:
'Zion said, "The LORD has forsaken me, the
Lord has forgotten me." Can a mother forget
the baby at her breast and have no compassion
on the child she has borne? Though she may
forget, I will not forget you! See, I have en-
graved you on the palms of my hands; your
walls are ever before me.'

Isaiah
49:14-16

The Exile and the Return

The great majority of Israelites were tran-
sported to Babylon, whilst the few who
remained decayed into anarchy and eventually
migrated *en masse* to Egypt. Those in Babylon
did not find life so hard as they might have
expected. They were permitted to live and
work together. They had some freedom of
assembly, and in Babylon many of the institutions of Judaism took shape – the synagogue,
the dedication to the Law, the rabbinical
system, and the preservation of the sacred
books which were eventually to form the Old
Testament.

Daniel 5

Ezra 1:1-8

In 539 the armies of Cyrus the Persian entered the city of Babylon and that great empire collapsed. Persia was now the ruling power. Within a year the Jews had been given leave to return to Jerusalem, to rebuild their temple, and to pray for the good of the Persian Empire (cf. Amos 9:11-15). It is not surprising that Jews became mercenaries in the Persian army. Near the Aswan Dam archaeologists found a Jewish army barracks with accompanying settlement.

539

538

Ezra 3

Ezra 5

The return from the exile turned out to be a rather poor affair. There was no great mass return, people dribbled back over the years. They met vicious opposition from the Samaritans and others, and could only get the foundations laid, and the altar raised, before they were obliged to stop. It would be another 20 years before the prophets Haggai and Zechariah appeared to enthuse the people to complete the building.

Ezra 7
Nehemiah 1-2

Nehemiah 5

Malachi 3:14-15

Subsequently Ezra the scribe and later Nehemiah the civil governor arrived. Nevertheless there were grave problems. Many had to mortgage their fields due to bad crops, and some of the wealthier Jews exploited the poverty of their compatriots to their own financial benefit. Intermarriage with foreigners caused grave difficulties. Finally the mass of the people took to skepticism. They said, 'It is futile to serve God. What did we gain by carrying out his requirements and going about like mourners before the LORD Almighty? But now

458

445

400

we call the arrogant blessed. Certainly the evil-
doers prosper, and even those who challenge
God escape.'

Sadly, the history of Israel ends with a curse.
The last verse of the Old Testament says: 'See,
I will send you the prophet Elijah before that
great and dreadful day of the LORD comes. He
will turn the hearts of the fathers to their
children, and the hearts of the children to their
fathers; or else I will come and strike the land
with a curse.'

Malachi
4:5-6

At first glimpse this might seem like disaster,
but let the reader reflect a little. In the modern
TV mini-series the plot is set early on, but the
action seems largely to frustrate the plot. The
wrong man is convicted of the crime, and for a
long time frustration continues. As the end
approaches the last but one episode seems to
leave us in an impossible situation as the wrong
person suffers. Yet we know that this is not
the end, that marvellously the last episode will
unravel the mystery, the righteous will be
vindicated and evil will be destroyed.

In like manner the first act of God's drama ends
in seeming disaster. There is an intermission
of 400 years, but then the second act is worked
out in the glorious fulfilment of God's purpose
in Christ. All that Israel was meant to be and
do would be worked out in him.

Why bother with this History?

Israel believed that God's face had smiled on her through her history. But Israel's history failed to achieve what God desired. On a recent air flight from Israel I read through the Passover Haggadah, a Jewish service for the family on the annual night of the Passover, in which Jews retell and relive the Exodus. In this service there is much about God's choosing of Israel, but it is all inward looking. God saves Israel for her own benefit and nothing more. There is not a word which speaks of Israel's calling to serve mankind.

The biblical concept of Israel's election was rather that she had been chosen in order to be a blessing to the nations. God had said it so clearly to Abraham: 'all peoples on earth will be blessed through you' (Gen. 12:3), and this is the basic plot of the Old Testament. God always works from the particular to the universal.

People are often perplexed, to think that God chose Israel in some special way, distinct from what he might have done with the rest of mankind. The answer lies in the fact that God always starts with the particular. The first eleven chapters of the Bible start by painting a picture of God dealing with the universal, in which the constant theme is the collapse of the system – the family of Adam, Noah's generation, the tower of Babel – all universal systems breakdown. So God began again with an individual, Abraham. But not Abraham as an end in himself. Not Abraham's family, clan, tribe, nation, as an end in itself, but as a means to an end.

Historically the plan for Abraham's people failed in two senses. First externally. They never reached out to other peoples. They missed their vocation as God's messengers to the nations. On the other hand they also failed internally, which is what the book of Amos is all about. Israel's failure to be God's people, to be a light to the nations, leaves us expecting something greater in the fullness of time.

And so it was. Jesus came, rooted in an historic place and time. He came as a particular man, living and dying in a particular set of circumstances, but God's aim in him was to achieve within history what Israel failed to achieve – the creation of a godly people, who would also take God's message of salvation to the nations. Do we as Christians measure up to that plan?

2

Amos the Tekoan

The Geography of Amos and of Israel

I once heard a St. John's Ambulance man point to an example of artificial respiration in the Bible. The widow woman of Shunem, whose son had a heat stroke, asked Elisha to restore him to life. Elisha stretched himself out over the boy, 'mouth to mouth', the body turned warm, and life was restored (2 Kings 4:34-35). Here was a clear case of artificial respiration.

I quietly made the observation that from Shunem at the foot of Mt. Moreh across the Plain of Jezreel to where Elisha was at Carmel was a distance of about 28 kilometres (17.5 miles). The journey would have taken her at least the rest of the day by donkey, she would have rested the night, and it would be a whole day before they returned to Shunem. By that time the boy would be stone cold. No artificial respiration here!

This incident demonstrates a common difficulty among Bible readers – a lack of perspective of the physical landscape in which the Bible story happened. It is in many ways an amiable error, likely to produce little more than a smile from the listener who knows a little of the lay of the land of the Bible.

What do you make of the following passage from Isaiah 10:28-30?

> They enter Aiath;
>   they pass through Migron;
>   they store supplies at Michmash.
> They go over the pass, and say,
>   'We will camp overnight at Geba.'

49

Ramah trembles;
Gibeah of Saul flees.
Cry out, O Daughter of Gallim!
  Listen, O Laishah!
Poor Anathoth!
Madmenah is in flight;
  the people of Gebim take cover.
This day they will halt at Nob;
  they will shake their fist
at the mount of the Daughter of Zion,
  at the hill of Jerusalem.

Probably 95+% of readers are totally confused by this passage. Without geographical knowledge it is almost unintelligible. Plotting these places on a map, however, makes them come alive. It shows that they describe the march of an army as it approaches Jerusalem, but you would never know it without so doing. I have stood at Geba and looked across to Michmash. Sure enough there is a ravine. The army is exhausted by the time it gets across, so the decision is taken to camp for the night in Geba. Their arrival provokes panic in the nearby towns and villages through which they will pass the next day en route to Jerusalem. Refugees flee from these places to find a safer haven further away.

The next day the army would be on the march to cover the six crow miles to Jerusalem eventually halting at Nob, the priestly village which lay below the city walls – and Jerusalem knows that its end is in sight.

In the same way the book of Amos has many geographical references, which may be lost to the casual reader.

Amos the Tekoan

I have called Amos 'the Tekoan' for in that village he was born and raised. You can trace it on a map south of Jerusalem and Bethlehem, a mile or two east of the main north-south highway. It stands on a hill on the edge of the Judean desert. From here can be seen Jerusalem, twelve miles distant to the north, and the Dead Sea, twelve terrifying miles distant across the desert canyons to the east, which plunge 4,000 feet to the lowest place on earth. Behind the Dead Sea can be seen the hills of Moab. Tekoa is a typical small, isolated village of Judah. Villages to the north of Jerusalem were generally more pleasant, surrounded by cultivated fields. The rough, stony, tuft grass area around Tekoa was better suited to sheep farming, and it is to this that Amos dedicated his time.

The only event of historic importance relating to Tekoa happened about 80 years before Amos' birth. It must have been retold many times in the village during his childhood. King Jehoshaphat in Jerusalem received news that the combined troops of Moab, Ammon and Edom had massed at Ein Gedi on the shores of the Dead Sea, and were heading up through the Judean mountain passes to Tekoa. This was a totally unexpected ruse and would be exceedingly dangerous for Tekoa, Bethlehem and Jerusalem. After much prayer the Judean army set out to confront them, but then received news that on the desert road to Tekoa the enemy armies had been mysteriously ambushed, many of them slaughtered, and the armies thrown into confusion and rout. By the time the Israelites got to them the Moabites were in total disarray.

From Tekoa to Bethel, where Amos preached, will have been a fascinating journey, both from the physical aspect and from the historic. Many a traveller of biblical times passed down this road. Abraham, the very first Bible traveller, entered the land, probably up the Wadi Fariah ravine from mid-Jordan, and arrived at Shechem where the road begins. He continued his journey down the road, passing Tekoa, until he reached Hebron and Beersheba, both located on this road, the only north-south way in these mountains. Beersheba is its terminus.

Centuries before Amos, Jacob and his family, with the pregnant Rachel, journeyed down this road from Shechem. It seems that as they passed Ramah her labour pangs came upon her. No health service hospital in those days, so they were forced to press on.

Their journey took them past the walls of Jerusalem, but the Jebusite stronghold was hostile and they pressed on five miles to Bethlehem. Before they could reach that town the baby boy, Benjamin, was born and Rachel died giving birth to him.

100 years before Amos Elijah fled down this road from the anger of the evil Jezebel, whilst seven centuries later Joseph and Mary travelled down it with their donkey to Bethlehem to be registered by the Romans. Amos will have walked through Bethlehem from Tekoa. When he reached Jerusalem he passed by the city at the north-west corner of the hill on which it was located.

Did he go into the city? He must have done so on many occasions in the past, and will have visited the temple to join in the worship of the people. Some time later he would pass the hill of Gibeah to his right. Perhaps he spied the ruins of the army barracks which King Saul built on its heights?

Geography in Amos' Book
There are many references to geographic locations in Amos. Here are a few.

From Jerusalem to Carmel. 1:2 pictures the Lord roaring like a lion from Jerusalem and his roar reaches to Carmel in the far north-west of the country. If you look at the map you will see that his roar passes across the territory of the northern nation, Israel, which is the main point of Amos' preaching in that land. When Amos preaches, God is roaring. Moreover, whilst Jerusalem is the centre for the worship of the Lord, Carmel represents the land of the false god Baal, on whose territory to the north (modern Lebanon) one looked down from its heights.

The Surrounding Nations. From 1:3 to 2:3 the Lord utters his condemnation of the surrounding nations. There is not the space here to engage in a description of these, but if you look at a Bible map you will see that they encircle Israel. Their condemnations seem designed by Amos to produce a chorus of 'Amens' from the Israelites as all their traditional enemies come under the whiplash of divine wrath, but the intention of the prophet was to draw a geographical noose around the neck of the Israelites in order to show, 2:4-8, that the same divine wrath was directed against them. As we have already noted, no chorus of 'Amens' greeted this!

Walking in the Desert. Sometimes the geographic reference in Amos eludes us. For example, *Do two walk together unless they have agreed to do so?* (3:3), seems a strange, even meaningless, question to us. But in the Judean desert around Tekoa, one doesn't simply bump into somebody and start walking together. If you see two people walking together in the desert, you assume they have made a prior arrangement to do so. This is part of a cause and effect argument, and fits perfectly.

Ashdod, Egypt, and the mountains of Samaria, 3:9. Ashdod was one of the five cities of the pagan Philistines, traditional enemies of Israel, who still inhabited the area to the south-west. The Egyptians lay to the far south-west. Samaria is the area in the heart of the central hill country of Israel. These two pagan nations are invited to assemble on the mountains of Samaria to see the terrible evil which prevails in the Lord's country, and among the Lord's people!

Cows of Bashan, 4:1. Bashan is located to the east of the Sea of Galilee, apparently famous for its fat cows, though I must confess that in four trips through the area I have not been impressed by the size of their modern representatives. Amos compares the obese women of Samaria to the fat cows of Bashan, because they themselves pressure their husbands to exploit the poor people so they might enjoy a more luxurious life-style. Not a very nice thing to say, I hear you murmur, but then these women were not very 'nice' toward those they despised and exploited.

False Worship Centres are referred to at various points by Amos
– Bethel and Gilgal (4:4); Beersheba (5:5). These places had holy
associations in Israel's past. Bethel had been the first place at
which Abraham had built an altar to the Lord, and the place where
Jacob dreamed of a staircase sweeping up to heaven (Gen. 32).
Gilgal, located near Jericho, was Joshua's base camp throughout
his wars with the Canaanites, and it was here that Saul, the first
king of Israel, was crowned (1 Sam. 11: 14-15). Beersheba had
holy associations as the place where Abraham had lived. Another
two cult centres are mentioned in 8:14, Samaria and Dan.

Calneh, Hamath and Gath, 6:2. This passage is directed to the
'notable men', the nation's leaders. They are called on, in the
midst of their luxury life-style, to consider what has happened to
these cities. Calneh was associated with the important town of
Arpad, 20 miles south-west of the modern city of Aleppo. Arpad
was sacked by Sargon II in 720, and presumably Calneh with it.
The next year Sargon conquered Hamath, located on the Orontes
River, north of Damascus. Around this time Philistine Gath also
fell, probably at the same time as Ashdod did (Isa. 20:1). These
should stand as a solemn warning to the leaders of Israel, *Are you
better than those kingdoms?* These events, however, belong to a
time 40 years after Amos, so he may be referring to attacks of
which we are ignorant. The meaning, however, remains the same.

Lo Debar and Karnaim, 6:13. There were cities with these names
to the east of the Jordan, but they were Israelite cities, so that it is
difficult to see why Israel should boast of having taken them.
Place names often had significance, so that it is possible to translate
this verse: 'You who are jubilant over a *nothing* and boast, "Have
we not won *power* by our own strength?" ' This would then be
mockery of Israelite claims to power, perhaps in some recent
victory.

Lebo-Hamath and **Arabah, 6:14.** A foreign nation is soon to
attack the land, *they will oppress you all the way from Lebo-*

Hamath to the valley of the Arabah. This is a vaster area than the usual boundaries of Israel, 'from Dan to Beersheba', equivalent to British, 'from Land's End to John O'Groats', or American, 'from coast to coast'. It seems rather to refer to the extent of the Israelite territory which had in recent times extended much further north to the territory north of Damascus, and far south to the Gulf of Akaba, precisely under Jeroboam and Uzziah, the two kings of Amos' time.

The Great Deep, 7:4. Another elusive reference. Amos sees a vision in which a ball of fire swept over the land. The Great Deep is the Mediterranean Sea, with the ball of fire sweeping across it, drying it up by the fierceness of its heat, and hurtling over Israel to devour it completely.

The Wider Geographic Perspective

We are now in a position to widen our view of the geography of that land where kings, priests and prophets lived and moved, where Jesus travelled widely. We said in the Introduction that the spiritual message of Scripture is intelligible apart from a knowledge of the geography. Thank God for this. Yet much of Scripture is at least not entirely intelligible, and just occasionally quite confusing, if we have no understanding of the geography of Palestine.

Palestine as a Land Bridge. One of the most important things to note is that Israel stood as a land bridge between great centres of empire and commerce on what historians call The Fertile Crescent, because it is shaped like a crescent between the Euphrates and the Nile. To the south lay the great empire of Egypt, to the north, that of the Hittites, and to the east the empires of Assyria, Babylonia, and Persia. These green and fertile lands were favoured by the Euphrates and Tigris rivers to the east, and the Nile to the south-west.

This factor was to affect Israel *culturally*. She was heir to three cultures:

1. **Mesopotamia.** Abraham travelled from Ur in Sumeria, through Syria to Canaan.[1] He will have been well-versed in the culture of the east, and it is significant that the culture of the Canaanites was basically derived from Mesopotamia, home of the original Sumerian people.

2. **Egypt.** The founder of Israel's faith, Moses, was trained in all the wisdom of Egypt. Egyptian influence is found in striking parallels to the tabernacle, and the similarities in their wisdom literature.

3. **Canaan.** Israel conquered Canaan, but did not stamp out the Canaanite influence. There are similarities in many aspects of Israelite life – language, sacrifices, feasts, temple structure, etc. Other features were thoroughly negative and destructive, e.g. Baalism.

Commercial influences were great. The main trade route between the great centres of empire lay through Israel. These empires wanted the trade routes maintained open and would station garrisons along them for that purpose, on occasions Gaza, Megiddo and Beth Shan were Egyptian garrisons. At other periods the Israelites themselves took advantage of their favourable position to assert their economic dominance, as in the time of Solomon.

International diplomacy passed through Palestine. Astonishingly, even before the coming of the Israelites, letters were being sent from dependent Canaanite cities in Palestine, written to the Egyptian court, in the Accadian cuneiform writing of Mesopotamia. Evidently there was a language of international diplomacy long before the Israelites invaded the land. We need to reflect on that for a moment. Even before the coming of the Israelites, there was international diplomacy and a common diplo-

---

[1] There is a difficulty in titling the land, since it was Canaan before the Israelites possessed it, then became 'the land of Israel'. It has so often been called Palestine over the past 2,000 years that it is hard to avoid calling it that today. Hence all three descriptions occur here.

matic language between the countries which surrounded Canaan. In fact, there was even a complete alphabetic writing in use. Let us not consider ancient peoples as so many ignorant children.

Warfare passed through Israel. When the great empires were in conflict, it became the staging ground for their armies, which swept across this land bridge and often destroyed whatever was in their path. Often they demanded tribute from the small states, and would use these as buffer zones against their enemies.

Among those powers which crossed or invaded the Canaanite/ Israelite land bridge in Old Testament times, of whom we have records from biblical and archaeological sources, are the *Egyptian Pharaohs*: Seti I, Thutmose III, Ramesses II and III, Merneptah, Shishak, Tirhakah and Neco; the *Mesopotamian kings*: Sargon of Accad, Shalmaneser III, Tiglath-Pileser III, Shalmaneser V, Sargon II, Sennacherib, Ashurbanipal, Nebuchadnezzar, Cambyses.

An excellent example of the way in which Palestine served as a land bridge between the two great centres of empire is found in 2 Kings 23:28-24:10.

23:29 The Egyptian Pharaoh, Neco, moved to aid Assyria against Babylon.

23:29-30 Josiah of Judah rushed his army to Megiddo to stop Neco, and was killed. The year was 608 BC.

23:33 Neco ruled over all Palestine. He called the new Judean king to 'Riblah in the land of Hamath', i.e. Syria, deposed him and replaced him with a puppet king, Jehoiakim. Egypt now dominated all Palestine. It was not to last long.

24:1 Four years later (604 BC), Babylon, having defeated Assyria at Carchemish the previous year, established its power in Palestine.

24:7 Egypt is in decline and driven out of Palestine. Jehoiakim swore allegiance to Nebuchadnezzar.

24:1 After three years, Jehoiakim rebelled against Babylon, possibly under Egyptian influence.

24:10 His revolt was crushed, and Babylon achieved total control of the area.

The Roads which Crossed Israel

As a natural land-bridge between the Empires, important highways crossed through her territory.

1. The Via Maris. The 'Way of the Sea' is the oldest known highway in world history, and certainly the most important road in the ancient Near East. From the Euphrates River it turned south to Damascus. From that city it continued south till it reached the hills of Bashan which it was forced to skirt because of the swampy character of the land, the Huleh basin. Another road ran down the eastern side of the hills of Lebanon. The two routes joined at the important city of Hazor. It then skirted the north-west edge of the Sea of Galilee, the scene of Jesus' later ministry, and pierced into the heart of Galilee via the Arbel Pass, very near modern Tiberias. In this respect Galilee was unique among the three major areas of Israel – Galilee, Samaria and Judea – since she was much more exposed to the march of armies and of caravans of other nations, and so is called by the prophet (Isa. 9:1).

From Galilee the road turned south to travel between Mt. Tabor and the north-west side of Mt. Moreh, crossing the Jezreel Plain via Ophra (Afula today) to the pass between the mountains at Megiddo. This city controlled all movement through the pass. From Megiddo the road ran to the coastal plain. Since it was often marshy, the road hugged the slopes of the central hills. Eventually it passed through Philistine territory to quit Palestine at Gaza. Since Gaza would be the last town en route to Egypt, an Egyptian garrison was often located in that area.

2. The King's Highway. This road travelled directly south from Damascus, using the hill country to the east of the Jordan. It passed through Bashan, including its main city of Ashtoreth-Karnaim, then through Gilead and the city of Ramoth-Gilead. It carried on via Rabbah, capital of Ammon, via Heshbon and Dibon, cities of Moab, and finally through Edomite territory to the port at Ezion-Geber (modern Eilat). At various points one could leave this road to enter Israel, Judah or the Sinai. From Eilat one could continue south to the important spice routes from Sheba (Yemen).

A good example of the use of this road is found in Ezekiel, where Nebuchadnezzar is pictured travelling down it until he *will stop at the fork in the road, at the junction of the two roads*... One road goes east to Rabbah, capital city of the Ammonites, the other goes west to Jerusalem. Nebuchadnezzar consults idols and a liver (like reading tea leaves), to decide which way he will turn, and Jerusalem is chosen (Ezek. 21:18-23).

3. The Road through the Central Hill Country.
We have already noted this road, because it was the road which Amos took from Tekoa to Bethel. I mentioned there that it started at Shechem in the north, but really it started further north.

One of the most important features of the geography of Israel is the Jezreel Plain, which the Way of the Sea crossed from Ophra to Megiddo. If you go directly south from Ophra, the road goes into a basin below the hills and eventually reaches modern Jenin (biblical Ein Gannim). Here is where the north-south road starts, going up into the hills through the Pass of Ibleam (where King Ahaziah of Judah was shot down by Jehu's chariot archers, 2 Kings 9:27), past Taanach to the west, and on across the Dotham Plain. The road travelled through mountainous terrain until it reached the city of Samaria, capital of the northern kingdom.

Shortly after Samaria the road joins the Shechem Valley road, which runs west from Shechem to the modern Arab town of Tulkarm. Turning east we reach Shechem, which lay in the heart of the northern territory, occupied today by the Arab city of Nablus, the largest city in the West Bank. All roads lead to Shechem, whether from the north and west, as already mentioned, northeast from Beth Shan, east from mid-Jordan up the Wadi Fariah Pass, or from the south.

Turning south the road moves along the watershed. Rain falling to the east runs down the gullies into the Jordan, whilst rain to the west finishes its journey in the Mediterranean. It is of interest here to note that there is only one specific geographic location given in the Old Testament, located on this road. In general the writers supposed that the reader knew the location of every place mentioned. The one exception is Shiloh in Judges 21:19, where we read: *There is the annual festival of the LORD in Shiloh, to the north of Bethel, and east of the road that goes from Bethel to Shechem, and to the south of Lebonah.* The old north-south road is virtually intact today, and after we travel south from Shechem, having just passed Lebonah to our right, we encounter the road, after 3,000 years, on our left going into the hills to Shiloh, the first sanctuary of Israel.

From here the road passes through very tortuous, tight-knit hills. This road was infested with brigands until the British authorities established a police station there in the 1920s. Having negotiated this area we pass through or near many towns and villages found in the biblical story – Bethel, Mizpah, Rama, Gibeah – whilst to the east we see, a mile or two off the main road, Ai, Michmash and Geba, and to the west, Gibeon, and Nabi Samwill ('Prophet Samuel's hill' in Arabic).

Arriving at Jerusalem the ancient road skirted the top of the Ben Hinnom Valley, and one can imagine many a Hebrew traveller before David took the city, looking up nervously at the Jebusite stronghold as he hurried by. The road took him south through Bethlehem, near which is the Church of St. Elijah, where tradition says Elijah rested whilst fleeing from Jezebel. Here too is the shrine to Rachel who died as she approached the town.

South from Bethlehem the road passes Tekoa and heads for Hebron, famed for its association with the patriarch Abraham, and so on to Beersheba on the edge of the desert.

The Joppa, Jericho, Rabbah road. The main east-west road in biblical times ran from Joppa, the only port on the coast, past Gezer, through the Plain of Aijalon, climbed the Beth-Horon Pass and reached the heights at Gibeon. Gibeon was a strategic location, and this almost certainly explains why the Gibeonites were so anxious to gain a special relationship with Israel when they invaded the country under Joshua (Joshua 9). They will have reckoned that their strategic location would mean that they would be next on the list for invasion. Many centuries later, in 1917, when General Allenby's British army captured Gaza and streamed along the coast and up this road, it was only at Gibeon that they were finally halted for a couple of weeks by the Turks.

During the Arab-Israeli war of 1948 the Arabs dominated the road from the sea-coast to Jerusalem, so Israeli engineers built a new road, which is the modern road you travel up from Tel Aviv.

Places worth Knowing

Jerusalem is the most famous city of Israel, so it is a little difficult to think that for, at the very least, 300 years it did not belong to the nation. A small tribe called the Jebusites held it whilst Israel carried on its business beneath the city's walls. It must at times have been fairly friendly with the Israelites, for the servant of a priest passing by its walls suggested: *Come, let's stop at this city of the Jebusites and spend the night* (Judg. 19:11), and King David was anxious to pay Araunah the Jebusite a fair price for buying the threshing floor on which the temple was to be built (2 Sam. 24:24).

After David had been king for seven years in Hebron, he decided that Jerusalem should be his new capital, for it was strategically located in little Benjamin between the large and often bitterly competitive tribes of Judah and Ephraim. It was a wise move, and he established it as the centre of government and of religion. The nation's temple was built there, and became the central focus of national worship. When the kingdom split in two on the death of Solomon, Jerusalem became the capital of the southern kingdom of Judah.

Shechem became the capital of the northern kingdom, Israel, at the division. It is the most natural capital in the land for, as we have seen, in the northern part all roads pass through the city. It lay in front of the two mountains of Ebal and Gerizim, on which the blessings and the curses were pronounced when the Israelites entered the land. Gerizim is said to offer the best vantage point from which to view the whole land.

Though it was the first capital, its usefulness was short-lived, for with the improvement of siege tactics Shechem became impossible to defend, as the two hills above her permitted her enemies the ability to fire at will into the city from above with deadly accuracy. Nevertheless, to this day Shechem is important, since it houses the largest town on the West Bank, Nablus, with a population of 100,000 Arabs. A traveller of the past century claimed to find 37 springs in the area, and its excavator called it the queen of Palestine.

Samaria became the new capital of the north in the province of the same name, being built by kings Omri and Ahab. The latter was said to have built an ivory palace there (presumably decorated, not built, with ivory) and pieces of ivory have been found in the ruins of the city. The Bible says that it was built on an unused hill overlooking a valley, and excavations, passing through Roman, Greek, Persian, and Assyrian levels, reached bedrock after Ahab's city had been excavated. In its strategic position overlooking the valley, through which all traffic from the north passed, and from which direction came most foreign opposition, Samaria could control all movements.

Its walls were about 30 feet wide, and its gate was so well crafted that it took the might of the great Assyrian army three years' siege to achieve its surrender. Subsequent generations, Assyrians, Samaritans, Greeks and Romans, all used the massive walls which Ahab had built and simply built around them.

Megiddo is one of three major cities of Palestine which straddled the main highway between the empires. In fact it held a unique position. From the hill of Megiddo one looks out on an impressive scenario of biblical places: Mt. Carmel on the far left, ahead Nazareth and Mt. Tabor, to the right the Hill of Moreh and the Jezreel Valley which heads down to the Jordan, the Sea of Galilee, and Beth-Shan. Further to our right lies the city of Jezreel and the sweep of the hills leading up Mt. Gilboa and beyond to the central hill country. This is a breath-taking scene of Biblical history in its geographical setting.

Here at Megiddo Egyptian Pharaoh Thutmose III records he faced '300 kings' in battle and gained a decisive victory, amusingly describing the defenders letting down sheets from the city walls for their soldiers to clamber up to safety. Here in the valley before us Deborah's army clashed with the 900 charioteers of the King of Hazor, which the flooding of the Kishon river immobilised (Judg. 4,5); here King Josiah tried to cut off Pharaoh Neco of Egypt (2 Kings 23:29-30); here in 1918 General Allenby fought a decisive battle against the Turkish army; and here is Armageddon, meaning the Hill of Megiddo, where *the kings of the whole world [are] gathered together to the place that in Hebrew is called Armageddon* (Rev. 16:16), for the last battle of the end times.

The 'mighty Kishon' today looks little more than a ditch, or at best a small stream, basically due to Israeli water control and fish farming.

Jezreel is located on the north-west spur of Mt. Gilboa, projected into the Jezreel Valley. It gained its fame from its association with the name of Ahab. Here this king built a winter retreat, away from the colder air of Samaria, so that at that time of the year it became a second capital. It was in this city that he cast his envious eyes on a little plot of land owned by a local citizen, Naboth. Egged on by his evil wife, Jezebel, a thoroughly pagan woman, who could never understand this Mickey Mouse kingdom she had married into, Naboth was accused of blasphemy, and together with his two sons was stoned to death, just so that Ahab could have his bit of land (1 Kings 21).

Shortly after, Jehu perpetrated a bloody massacre in this city. Ahab's grandson, Joram, got a nasty shock as he looked out toward the east from here. He saw his army general Jehu hurtling up the valley, *he drives like a madman* the watchers said. Joram, together with his cousin Ahaziah, king of Judah, went out to meet him, but soon realising his danger, turned heel and fled in his chariot. Jehu's arrow, however, shot Joram between the shoulders and he died (2 Kings 9).

Wait though, there is another sight we see from this mound. North-west of here lies the town of Nazareth, up in the hills. Jesus came down from those hills to make his journey to Jerusalem. When he reached Ophrah he faced the decision, whether to go directly south, pass Jezreel on his left, and climb up into the hills at the Pass of Ibleam, or to turn south-east, passing Jezreel on his right, and walking down through the valley to Beth-Shan and along either side of the Jordan River to Jericho, and thence to Jerusalem. Either way, and we know he took both, we can imagine him with a group of friends, relatives or disciples making his way past Jezreel.

There are so many other towns and villages which dot this land with holy and unholy associations. Among the Benjamite hills just north of Jerusalem there are considerable towns with biblical connections.

Bethel was the first place in which Abraham built an altar to the Lord. It was to Bethel that he returned after dismal moral failure in Egypt. Here his grandson, fleeing from his brother's fury, saw a vision of a staircase sweeping up to heaven, with angels ascending and descending on it. He called the place Bethel, the House of God (Gen. 32). Some centuries later the bad king Jeroboam, frightened that the people of his newly-founded nation would desert him for Jerusalem, built a rival temple in which false religion became endemic. It was at this very temple that our friend Amos proclaimed his tirade against the northern kingdom.

Mizpah is the town where eleven tribes came together to plan a war against the Benjamite tribe (Judges 20), and it was to become for a very short time the capital city after the fall of Jerusalem to the Babylonians in 586 BC. A long climb at the end of a tiring day took me to the top of Mizpah. I was intrigued by some very large man-made holes in the ground, with plastered rims. Returning home, my archaeology books informed me that these dated from biblical times and were cisterns for storing water. Some were three times larger than the house which stood over them.

Gibeah was the town which the Israelites attacked on the former occasion. It has the distinction of being the first capital of the country, with the title 'Gibeah of Saul'. It was in this town that David played his harp to the half-mad king. On the hill top of Gibeah, King Hussein of Jordan began to build a palace when his country ruled the West Bank, but the Israelis forced him out, and some years ago I wandered among its unfinished, decaying shell.

North of Gibeah lies **Ramah,** where Samuel had his residence, and from where he travelled to visit various centres to judge Israel: *But he always went back to Ramah, where his home was...* (1 Sam. 7:17). North of Ramah are the two villages of **Geba** and **Michmash,** facing each other across a sharp ravine. The latter was a Philistine garrison, and it was from Geba that Jonathan, Saul's son, crossed over the ravine to attack it with his armour bearer (1 Sam. 14). Later this ravine became the frontier between the northern and southern kingdoms, so that 'from Dan to Beersheba' became 'from Geba to Beersheba' (2 Kings 23:8).

Away from the hill-country, in an area called the Shephelah, south-east of Jerusalem, lies the city of **Lachish.** It is even less known to the average reader than Megiddo. Yet it was to Judah what Megiddo was to northern Israel, the second city of the country, important for its defence against attack from Egypt, but also strategic in a possible pro-Egyptian alliance against a northern attack. Both Sennacherib of Assyria and Nebuchadnezzar of Babylon crippled Lachish before turning their attention to Jerusalem. It was a centre of evil, for within 30 years of Amos' time the prophet Micah accuses Lachish of having been the source of Jerusalem's evil (Micah 1:13).

Some New Testament places are barely mentioned in the Old Testament. Nazareth is unknown and was probably little more than a hamlet. Even in New Testament times it was so insignificant that all secular writers of the age omit to mention it.

There are so many other things we could say about the geography of the land. We could talk about mountain ranges and rivers, streams and hills, valleys and gorges, caves and hiding places, but I must restrain myself. I had never understood how Elijah could hide himself for three years from the king's men who hunted for him, until I went to Israel and realised how easy it is for a person who knows the land well to hide himself. The fascination for the geography will be born out of our encounter with the Bible itself. It gives us the physical dimension within which Bible characters and events moved.

I will end with two final observations. First, if you take a compass and draw a series of concentric circles from Jerusalem, each circle representing 10 miles, or 10 kilometres, you will get a good idea of the physical proportions of Israel, and this will enable you to get things into perspective. For example, when Joseph went in search of his brothers he journeyed to Shechem, some 50 miles away, and then went on to Dothan, another 10 miles to find them. They had wandered 60 miles (95 kilometres) from home in order to find grazing pastures for their sheep! This in itself serves to remind us that Palestine lies on the edge of the desert, and whilst the winter rains provide fertility, the blasting summer heat turns the land brown by June and grazing land is sparse.

The other thing to notice is that whilst distances by modern standards are short, travel is very slow. Joseph and Mary will have walked for three days from Nazareth to Bethlehem, and she was in an advanced state of pregnancy. In contrast I have travelled in a taxi from Jericho to Jerusalem in 20 minutes, admittedly doing 80 mph. The bus ride from Tel Aviv, Joppa of biblical times, is 40 minutes. We must slow this down to the pace of a donkey! Three miles an hour.

These two elements, relative smallness and journey times which would have been 10-20 times longer than today, will considerably affect our understanding of some events in the Bible.

3

Amos the Tekoan Shepherd

Bible Culture Shock

Travellers abroad testify to suffering culture shock when encountering people who think and act differently from those of their own nation. I have known young people go to the mission field fired up with enthusiasm, but so profoundly shocked by the difference in culture, that they have not been able to 'hack it'.

The new Bible reader also suffers a form of culture shock. I well remember my first encounter with John 13. Three things in the chapter puzzled me enormously. In the first place I was confused by the very act of washing someone's feet, hardly a very 'civilized' thing to do. Indeed, Jesus commanded the disciples that they were to continue washing one another's feet as a sign of discipleship. Was this required of me also? Then there was this business of John 'leaning on Jesus' breast', which sounded like a very effeminate act. Finally, there was the statement of Jesus, identifying the one who would betray him as the one who would dip bread with him in the food.

Consultation with a good commentary began to unravel these strange goings-on. Washing one another's sandalled feet on arrival from the dusty roads, was a common act of consideration for your guests. At a special meal people did not sit at table (in spite of Leonardo's picture of the Last Supper), but reclined on couches (as Amos makes clear, 6:4), so that John's head would naturally approach the chest of Jesus as he leaned back to talk to him.

As for my third problem, it would appear I am not the only one puzzled by this, for in AD 1481 Meshullam ben R. Menahem, an Italian Jew visiting Jerusalem, complains of the same practice: 'The Moslems and also the Jews of this place are pigs at their eating. They all eat out of one vessel with their fingers, without a napkin, just as the Cairenes do, but their clothes are clean.' He also suffered from culture shock, but who is to say which is the right way to eat?

Amos – only a Shepherd?

Our reaction on reading that Amos was a shepherd will be a measure of the difference between his culture and ours. We shall probably react by considering that his position was rather low on society's scale of values.

However, two things need to be said. First, he was probably a sheep farmer, rather than a herdsman. During the 16th century there were very large sheep farms in England, and wool was the basis of the economy. In such circumstances a sheep farmer will be a highly esteemed member of the community. So it was in the world of Amos.

Secondly, there are many references in the Bible to sheep farming, which show that to be a sheep farmer was an honourable position. The biblical writer has no embarrassment in explaining that the great king David was a sheep farmer before he became king. King Mesha of Moab was a sheep farmer even as king, and supplied a yearly tribute of 100,000 lambs, and the wool of 100,000 rams to the king of Israel (2 Kings 3:4). Furthermore, the function of kingship is often explained with figures of speech drawn from caring for sheep (Ezek. 34). Psalm 23 depends on considering shepherding as a well-known and respected way of life, worthy even for describing God's activity.

At the same time we must realise that a shepherd's life was not the idyllic picture which we often imagine – sitting on a hillside playing his flute whilst the sheep quietly munch on the grass. Jacob complained of his lot as a shepherd: *This was my condition: The heat consumed me in the daytime and the cold at night, and sleep fled from my eyes* (Gen. 31:40). Hardly a restful pursuit!

Similarities. Let's begin by noting that there are strong similarities between Amos' culture and our own. Here are examples from his book.

He describes Israel's enemies as being *tall as the cedars and strong as the oaks* (2:9). The modern reader will easily identify with these figures of speech, since cedars and oaks are well known to us for their height and strength, which is the point here. If we lived in the desert or in a tropical jungle, we might find that harder to understand.

He speaks of a bird falling into a trap or snare on the ground, of *a trap springing up from the earth* (3:5). Once again the culture is similar. From earliest time man has used traps to catch animals for food and clothing, and although there are serious questions today about humane forms of trapping, most of us will have seen traps in some form or other. Here the argument is based on the fact that if we hear a trap snap, we know that something has been caught.

When Amos asks, *Do horses run on the rocky crags? Does one plough there with oxen?* (6:12) he makes his point as easily with the modern reader as with the ancient. The answer is a firm 'No'. His argument is – just as these two illustrations strain credibility, so does the fact that God's chosen people should have perverted justice and righteousness. Point taken.

He uses an illustration taken from the act of measuring the true vertical of a wall with a plumb line, a lead on the end of a piece of string, common to bricklayers down through the centuries (7:8). The Bible uses this as the measuring of the rectitude of a life. So we hear the Lord saying through Isaiah: *I will make justice the measuring line and righteousness the plumb line* (28:17).

From these similarities we can see that there is no need to be overly scared by the idea of differences of culture, as though this would make the Bible incomprehensible to us. People have to eat, drink, dress, sleep, get sick, take medicine, be cured, marry, give birth, grow up and grow old, die and be buried, in any and every culture. Their similarities greatly outweigh their differences.

Dissimilarities. At the same time, we need to be aware of, and expect to find, important differences between all cultures, even when those cultures exist together in time. How much more when they are separated from each other by many hundreds of years, by history, geography and ways of thinking. Let us look at some difficulties in Amos.

We read of threshing *sledges having iron teeth* (1:3). Probably incomprehensible to most readers. After the wheat was harvested it was laid out on an exposed, flat surface and a 'machine' was run over it, in the form of a flat board with holes into which stones or bits of iron were wedged. These had the effect of separating the wheat from the straw. Amos uses this as a metaphor of extreme cruelty perpetrated by a marauding army.

The modern reader is likely to interpret the reference to the sword (1:11) as the Mediaeval European sword. Almost certainly it was the sickle shaped sword, from which we get the biblical reference to 'smiting with the edge of the sword'.

Garments seized in pledge (2:8) refers to the custom of giving one's coat as a guarantee against payment of a debt. It was the poor who incurred debts, and since poor people slept at night in the same clothes they wore during the day (I have seen and done the same in Indian huts in the Andes), and since however warm the day, on the edges of the deserts the night is cold, the taking of a man's cloak in pledge may well leave him without any warmth at night, and thus cause him serious difficulties, not to say dangers.

Saving a lamb's bones or torn ear (3:12) does not refer to some kind of culinary delicacy, but of the need for the employed shepherd to prove that he has not made off with his master's animal. If he could not prove this he was liable to make restitution to the owner for the value of the animal. Jacob complained to Laban: *I did not bring you animals torn by wild beasts; I bore the loss myself, and you demanded payment from me for whatever was stolen by day or night* (Gen. 31:39).

The *mourners summoned to wail* (5:16) are not the relatives and friends of the deceased, but the professional mourners who appear hundreds of years later in the Gospel account of the death of the synagogue ruler's daughter in Mark 5:38-50: *Jesus saw a commotion, with people crying and wailing loudly.* When Jesus tells them that there is no need to wail for the girl is only sleeping, they quickly turn to laughter and ridicule, which shows the mere professionalism and shallowness of their mourning.

Life in Old Testament Towns

We are now in a position to take a wider look at life in Amos' time. He gives us several glimpses of life in the towns. His birthplace, Tekoa, was something between a village and a town, being big enough to require fortification under King Rehoboam.

He constantly refers to the walls and gates of the towns. The divine destruction of the surrounding pagan people will centre on their walls and gates: *I will break down the gate ... send fire upon the walls* (1:5,7). Walls and gates constituted the main defensive strength of cities and towns.

Important towns were situated on natural hill tops, e.g. Gibeah and Samaria, or on mounds left by the debris of former towns, Beth Shan and Beersheba. These towns were supplied with massive defence systems. High walls and complicated gate systems were essential. The spies returning from Canaan reported that *the people who live there are powerful, and the cities are fortified and very large* (Num. 13:28). These required an enormous amount of manual labour as they had to be high (Deut. 1:28) and strong. Often very large stones were employed to build them. Layers of beaten earth were placed against lower levels, to form a steeply sloping bank, which was then covered with small stones to make it virtually impossible to run siege engines up them.

The walls of the city of Samaria, already referred to, with which Amos was familiar, were double walls, the outer being 1.8 metres wide, the inner 1 metre, and the roofed-in space between 7 metres. This made the total thickness of the protecting wall almost 10 metres wide. No doubt useful for chariot-racing, a lá James Bond or Ben Hur! It took the might of the Assyrian army three years of siege to produce the surrender of Samaria. Another facet of the defence was the placing of towers around the walls as lookouts and vantage points for attacking enemies who got too near the wall. Amos 4:3 speaks of breaches opened up in the walls. The objective of the attacking enemy was to weaken the wall and open up a gap in it, through which the marauding army could pour its troops. This then provides a suitable place through which prisoners can be led into captivity.

King Sennacherib of Assyria described his destruction of many towns of Judah, about 50 years after Amos' prophecies: *46 of his [Hezekiah's] strong walled towns and innumerable smaller villages in their neighbourhood I besieged and conquered by stamping down earth-ramps and then by bringing up battering rams, by the assault of foot soldiers, by breaches, tunnelling and sapper operations.* A graphic picture of Assyrian siege tactics.

Gates were potentially the weakest point in the city, so their construction was carefully planned to cause maximum problems for the attacker. The 'gate' was in fact a large area enclosing a public square in which much of the town's business and commerce flourished.

The full extent of the gateway at Dan was only recently discovered in 1993. It comprised two sets of three-gates, with an extensive area between the two. I walked up through and explored these gates in 1996. One has to think of the high walls which surrounded the whole area, providing shade from the heat of the sun (see drawing of the gateway on next page).

Here is a brilliant description of a city gate, that of Beirut, by a 19th century traveller, when Near Eastern cities had changed little from biblical times:

You observe that the gateway is vaulted, shady and cool. This is one reason why people delight to assemble about it. Again, the curious and vain resort thither to see and be seen. Some go to meet their associates; others, to watch for returning friends, or to accompany those about to depart; while many gather there

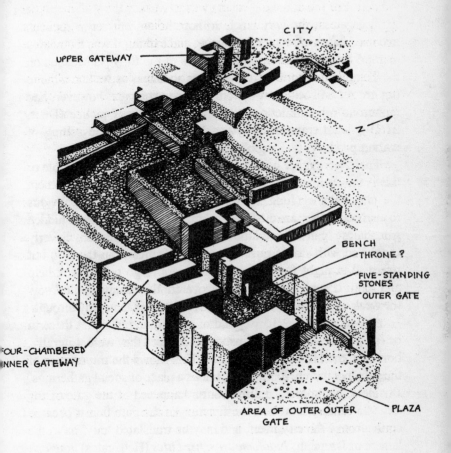

CITY

UPPER GATEWAY

N

BENCH
THRONE ?
FIVE-STANDING
STONES
OUTER GATE

FOUR-CHAMBERED
INNER GATEWAY

AREA OF OUTER OUTER
GATE

PLAZA

to hear the news, and to engage in trade and traffic. I have seen in certain places... the judge and his court sitting at the entrance of the gate, hearing and adjudicating all sorts of causes in the audience of all that went in and out thereat.[1]

The gates were very large, without hinges but set in sockets, and used heavy iron bars for closing and locking. I was fascinated in 1996 to note that the massive doors of the El Aqsa Mosque on the Temple Mound in Jerusalem have no hinges as we know them, but are set on sockets at bottom and top. The gate, however, had numerous other functions: the administration of justice (Deut. 21:19); legal transaction (Ruth 4:1,11); buying and selling of market products (2 Kings 7:1,18).

There were other gates which were very small. An example of this is the curious request of the Israelites for a man to show them the gate of Bethel (Judg. 1:23-25). The main gate would be obvious to anyone, so they are evidently asking him about the small, hidden gate. These 'gates' were little more than holes in the wall, cleverly concealed with stones pushed into them from within the city, but removed at night for scouts and foragers to go out to seek help and food. If such a gate were discovered, the enemy would know the weak part of the wall, and would soon smash their way through.

At Amos 5:10,12,15 we read of *courts*, and interpret these to be for the administration of justice, and indeed they were. Literally, however, the Hebrew says 'gates'. This shows the importance of the gate, not merely for defence, but as a place of social gatherings. Business, commerce, and the courts happened at the gate of the city. So fundamental was the function of the gate that it became equivalent to the city itself, and may be translated 'city' as in the lament of Jeremiah, *Judah mourns, her cities* (Heb. gates) *languish* (14:2). Within the city was a public square, a road leading from the gate to the governor's palace, and numerous alleyways leading to the homes of ordinary people.

---

[1]Thomson, *The Land and the Book* (Thomas Nelson, Edinburgh, 1896), p. 27f.

Housing. Housing is a major preoccupation of man, and of governments. In ancient Israel a clear distinction can be seen between the houses of the wealthy and those of the common people.

Houses of the Wealthy. Amos 5:11 speaks of stone mansions. The rich built large houses of the finest stone. Since the normal house had only three layers of stones from the foundation, and from there upwards were made of mud bricks, stone mansions speak of luxury. Amos was clearly angered by the building of stone mansions, for he says ... *you have built houses of hewn stone, but you shall not dwell in them...*, and the previous clauses show that they were able to achieve this standard of material prosperity only by the exploitation of the poor.

He also denounces their 'ivory houses' (3:15), i.e. heavily decorated with ivory. Ivory will have been very expensive, since it was imported from far-away India, and was highly prized by marauding troops as loot. A hundred years earlier King Ahab had set the trend by building a palace in Samaria inlaid with ivory (1 Kings 22:39). The historian chooses this as the one fact worthy of mention in the annals of Ahab's reign. It will still have been in use during Amos' time. Fragments of ivory from the ruins of Ahab's palace can be seen in the British Museum.

Wealthy people could also afford to have two houses, one in the highlands for use in the summer, and another in the lowlands to escape the cold of winter (Amos 3:15). A look at the geographical locations of Samaria and Jezreel will show the difference in altitude. In the New Testament period, Herod the Great built himself an important winter retreat in Jericho.

Houses of the Common People. The houses of the common people were very much humbler affairs, the most normal being the four-room house, of which there is a visible example today at the reconstructed Philistine town-house at Tell Qasile, in Tel Aviv. The same plan may be seen at Israelite sites as far away as Beersheba.

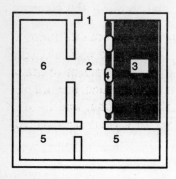

1 - Entrance from alleyway.
2 - Patio, open to the elements.
3 - "Living Room", covered only
      by an awning.
4 - Wooden posts set on stone base
      to support awning.
5 - Deposits.
6 - Family dormitory.

Here is a description:

The evening now was close and smoky. The lamp was lit, and
the ... doors shut. This house, like so many others I'd seen
already, held nothing more than was useful for living – no fuss
of furniture and unnecessary decoration – being as self-
contained as the ark. Pots, pans, the chairs and tables, the
manger and drinking-trough, all were of wood, stone or potter's
clay, simply shaped and polished like tools. At the end of the
day, the doors and windows admitted all the creatures of the
family: father, son, daughter, cousin, the donkey, the pig, the
hen, even the harvest mouse and the nesting swallow, bedded
together at the fall of darkness.[2]

The fascinating thing about this description is that it comes,
not from the Holy Land, but from Spain in the 1930s, as recorded
by Laurie Lee. It is a picture of life reduced to its simplest forms,
and British travellers to Israel in the last century paint very similar
pictures. The modern reader of the Nativity story usually assumes
that the 'manger' indicates that Jesus was born in a stable, but the

---

[2]Laurie Lee, *As I Walked Out One Midsummer Morning* (Heinemann, 1969), p. 61

above description shows that animals usually lived with the people, so he was almost certainly born in a house, but a house of the poorest people.

Provisions. Food had to be stored in the city, both in times of peace, and even more in times of war. A deep and wide silo, dug in the ground, permitted the storage of a large amount of grain and other cereals, whilst store-rooms have been found, identifiable both by their unnatural length and short breadth, and by the numerous jars found in them. These jars, of various sizes, stored water, wine, nuts, wheat and barley, olives and other fruits.

Water is man's most fundamental need. In a country on the edge of the desert this was perhaps the biggest headache of all. Cities were located near to a main highway, but also near to a water supply. However, as the city was set on a hill, this water supply became precarious in a time of siege. For this reason very elaborate systems involving shafts and tunnels were evolved in order to reach underground springs or wells from within the city walls.

Large cisterns were also common. Cisterns were often larger than the house above them. The visitor to the Temple Mound in Jerusalem is usually unaware that there are some 37 cisterns built into the mound beneath his feet. As he faces the El Aqsa Mosque he is standing a few yards from the Great Sea Cistern which could hold two million gallons. At Massada you can stand inside massive cisterns. Often pools were built within the city, the two referred to in the Gospels being the Pool of Bethesda and the Pool of Siloam.

Hygiene. Looking at the diagram of the houses of the common people, the reader is tempted to ask, 'Where's the toilet?' Whilst sewage systems are found in wealthy houses, most of the houses of the common people in a city had no refuse system. My wife-to-be and I were visiting a small town in Bolivia, when she needed a toilet. She insisted that I ask one of the locals, but I pointed out

that this would be useless as there would not be one. Finally I
succumbed and asked two men in the public square. They laughed
heartily, pointing out, 'Why do you need a toilet with all these
fields around!'

So also in Israel. In peace the people would simply go out into
the fields, but during a war refuse was tipped over the city wall! It
is curious and amusing to note that the only gate in Jerusalem
which still today retains its biblical name is the Dung Gate.
Hygienic conditions were vastly inferior to modern times, and
during a siege, with thousands more crowding into the city for
refuge, disease often broke out, and more would die from plagues
than from the enemy.

Crafts. Crafts flourished in the city. The typical form of industry
was the craftsman's shop. Among those found in the Old Testament are weavers, fullers, tailors, leather and metal workers, and
spice makers. All of these will have worked in their own houses,
to which the people would go to buy. In Jeremiah 18 the prophet
is told to go down to the potter's house. The potter worked in the
covered awning area of his house courtyard. Pottery was to the
world of Amos what tin was in the first half of this century, and
what plastic is to man in the second half, i.e. a cheap and
disposable, but very useful implement.

Burial. This could not take place within the limited confines of
the city, so had to be carried out in a nearby location. When General
Gordon identified what he thought was the hill of Golgotha in
Jerusalem, he reasoned that there must be a cave-tomb nearby,
and on digging his workmen found precisely that, today called
The Garden Tomb. However, had the good General known it, he
would have found such tomb caves almost anywhere he might
dig in the vicinity of an Israelite town. Indeed there are a good
number of burial caves on the other side of the 'Golgotha' hill
cave.

The limestone hills of the Holy Land often hide a honeycomb

of natural or man-created caves, for example in the Kidron and Ben Hinnom Valleys outside Jerusalem. Pre-Israelite people buried their dead with furniture, weapons and pottery, obviously for use in the hereafter, but Israelite graves are usually simple, almost devoid of material things.

Village Life

The biblical village was distinguished from the towns inasmuch as they were not walled. In some cases a village was larger than a town, though in most cases they were no bigger than modern hamlets. The town was surrounded by a wall which penned the people in and placed severe restrictions on population growth. The village, on the other hand, could expand considerably.

Villages were often grouped as 'daughters' (Num. 21:25, in Hebrew) around the city on which they depended politically and economically (Josh. 15:32, etc.). During a time of warfare they would retreat to the walled city, to live with relatives. Sometimes warfare was so widespread that *village life ceased in Israel* (Judg. 5:7). Despite its dependence on the city, a village might have its own local government (Ruth 4:2), and often a shrine or sacred place.

Life centred around agriculture, which can be graphically illustrated from its use in many figures of speech and parables.

Breaking ground (Jer. 4:3), which Jeremiah uses as a figure of repentance.

Sowing – Parable of the Sower (Mark 4:1-20)

Harvesting – Parable of the Weeds (Matt. 13:24-30)

Threshing (Isa. 28:23-29)

Winnowing (Isa. 41:15-16)

Olives and vines are the two trees reproduced by Sennacherib's war artists, now in the Lachish Room in the British Museum, as most characteristic of the land. Olives are important even today in Israel. It is in fact the *King of Trees* (Judg. 9:8). There is a museum to the olive in Tel Aviv. Vineyards and olive groves are linked together (Deut. 6:11), as the most conspicuous feature of plant life. It was an important economic factor, regarded also as a symbol of beauty, strength, divine blessing, prosperity, and peace. Olive trees provide

1. Shelter from the burning sun, and a place for meditation;
2. Oil for lighting lamps, cooking, medicine, perfume, anointing;
3. Fresh, or pickled olives are eaten with bread;
4. Olive branches were used to create booths (Neh. 8:15);
5. The large pips were used for burning in portable household braziers;
6. The wood is still used for fine cabinet-making.

Another important tree is the vine, a symbol of Israel (Isa. 5:1-7). Grapes were brought by the spies (Num. 13) as an important and delightful aspect of the country the Israelites were called on to inhabit. The vine in fact became the outstanding symbol of Israel. Yet in all its Old Testament appearances it is used to point up, not the blessedness, but the unfruitfulness of the nation in terms of the establishment of justice and righteousness for all its inhabitants (Isa. 5:1-7). Ezekiel points out in chapter 15 of his book that the only usefulness of a vine is that it produces fruit, and its wood is useless even for making pegs. Jesus saw himself as the true fruitful vine, and saw his followers as those who would truly produce the fruits of righteousness (John 15:1-6).

Many other trees are mentioned in the Old Testament – acacia, almond, cypress, oak, palm, pine, sycamore and fig, for all of which you will find descriptions in Bible dictionaries

The Topsy-Turvy Seasons
On the next page is a calendar of the seasons, found in the ruins of Gezer and dating from the times of Solomon. It shows a fair degree of literacy among the early Israelites, since this clay tablet is recognised by archaeologists as a school tablet used by a country school master. The Egyptian Pharaoh had quite recently given this city to his daughter as a dowry on her marriage to Solomon.

THE GEZER CALENDAR[1]

His two months are (olive) harvest	*September/October*
His two months are planting (grain)	*November/December*
His two months are late planting	*January/February*
His month is hoeing up of flax	*March*
His month is harvest of barley	*April*
His month is harvest and festivity	*May*
His two months are wine testing	*June/July*
His month is summer fruit	*August*

It will be noted that according to this calendar the cereal harvest is celebrated in May, since harvesting has taken place in April. Rain falls in winter, January and February, and the fairly mild winter matures the plants well ahead of the northern European schedule. Thus we see that the climactic conditions of Israel made important differences in the seasonal year.

The most fundamental difference is that we think of nature dying in the winter, whilst they thought of nature dying in the summer. It is not the cold of winter which is most to be feared, but the blistering heat of summer. In Canaanite legend Baal died in the summer, and Mot (death) reigns. By the end of May Jerusalem is baked brown, whilst the winter rains of January and February cause life to abound. So the Bible speaks of protection from life's scorching heat (Psalm 121:6; Isa. 49:10; Rev. 7:16). Judgment is spoken of in terms of blistering heat, not freezing cold.

Wells and Springs

Water is often as precious as gold in a hot country. Fortunately Israel was well blessed with springs and wells. The former spring up at the foot of the hills, as does the Jordan from Mt. Hermon at Dan. The Battle of Aphek between Israel and the Philistines (1 Sam. 4) was almost certainly a battle for the control of the very

---

[1]Translation of W. F. Albright, *Ancient Near Eastern Texts*, Princeton University Press, 1969, p. 320.

important springs in that area, called today Rosh Ha'ayin, *the head of the springs.* Compare also the Spring of Harod, where Gideon gathered his forces at the foot of Mt. Gilboa. Wells are dug to reach underground water, which percolates through the rock. These were built mainly in the hill country or in the desert. Compare Jacob's well at Sychar (Shechem in Old Testament), Abraham's well at Beersheba. The well was often little more than a hole in the ground, though the lip of the well was sometimes formed by large worked stones. A large stone would be placed over the hole.

Wells, springs and cisterns lend themselves to illustrations of spiritual reality. Thus the Lord castigates the Israelites: *My people have committed two sins: They have forsaken me, the spring of living water, and have dug their own cisterns, broken cisterns that cannot hold water* (Jer. 2:13). There is a world of difference between a bubbling, lively spring and a cistern of stagnant water. I had a cistern in a country house in Bolivia, which had to have the leaves, dust, dirt, and not infrequently rats, raked off it, and the water boiled before we could drink it. Jesus must surely have had this contrast in mind when he sat at Sychar's well and described himself, not as a cistern, but as the *spring of water welling up to eternal life* (John 4:14).

So much more could be said about the life and culture of biblical times. You may wish to explore themes like marriage, polygamy, family and divorce, domestic service and slavery, land distribution rules, etc., all of which had their own peculiarly biblical dimensions. But here we must curtail our enthusiasm.

Dealing with Bible Culture Shock

Here are some suggestions for reducing Bible Culture Shock and improving your interpretation of the Old Testament. First, remember that study of biblical culture is not an end in itself. Some may find it fascinating, but for the majority of us it is a tool to the knowledge of, and encounter with, the Word of God in Scripture. It is not that the message of the Bible will not be intelligible if we are ignorant of the cultural context, but knowing it will greatly save us from being frustrated and irritated by cultural distractions.

Secondly, cultivate an awareness of the similarities between your own culture and biblical culture. There are many illustrations – water, dress, food, etc. – which are used in the Bible and which correspond with our own. These should be our starting point and enable us to proceed from the known to the unknown.

Thirdly, if at all possible have a good Bible Dictionary or commentary on the Bible book you are reading available. Bible dictionaries are meant to be dipped into when you need enlightenment on any aspect. They cover the whole range of cultural activities.

I had the good fortune in my youth to discover James Neil's *Everyday Life in the Holy Land* (published in 1953 by the Church Mission to Jews). I have read it through three times, and still consult it. Neil was the Anglican bishop of Jerusalem over 100 years ago, when life in the Holy Land was very little different from what it was in biblical times. His first-hand experience brings many cultural factors to life, and the book is illuminated by a series of vivid paintings. J. A. Thompson's, *Handbook of Life in Bible Times* (published in 1986 by IVP), is more technical and up-to-date, and very useful.

4

Amos the Thinker

'The end has come for my people Israel'

Amos was a man who snapped. At some point of his life he was
suddenly overcome with a powerful sense of call. He had been no
more than a sheep farmer and a harvester of figs (7:14), but *the
LORD took me from tending the flock and said to me, 'Go, prophesy
to my people Israel'* (7:15). It was as simple as that. One day he
was following his sheep in the hills of Tekoa, the next his bag
was packed and he was legging up north to denounce the evil
being practised in Israel. It has happened down through the
centuries in the same way to men like Peter, Paul, Luther, Wesley,
Carey, Spurgeon, and myriads more: the unerring conviction that
God has told you to go and preach. From that point life will never
be the same.

This man Amos was an angry man, angry with what he had
seen and witnessed in the north. Though he does not expressly
say so, he was so conversant with what was happening in the
north that we are sure he must have been there before, probably
selling his lambs, sheep's wool, and figs. What he saw made him
angry.

Amos describes his reaction in three words in 1:1: *what he
saw.* What he saw as he travelled around the northern kingdom
convinced him that God, the God in whom he believed, could not
tolerate this for long. One can imagine him returning home from
one such visit, his mind profoundly disturbed, and he experienced
a series of three visions (again, *what he saw),* which he relates in
7:1-9.

In the first vision he saw a swarm of locusts sweeping over the land and the year's harvest was destroyed in a few hours. Such 'plagues' of locusts spelt disaster, famine and starvation through several months of blistering summer heat, autumn and winter, till the spring once again produced a crop. In an agony of soul Amos pleaded with the Lord: *When they had stripped the land clean, I cried out, 'Sovereign LORD, Forgive! How can Jacob survive? He is so small!' So the LORD relented!*

In the second vision he saw a ball of fire sweeping over the Mediterranean, so fierce that it left that Sea completely dry, hurtling toward the hills of Samaria and Judah. Once again, *I cried out, 'Sovereign LORD, I beg you stop! How can Jacob survive? He is so small!' So the LORD relented.*

From these two visions we learn something of the heart of Amos, and the heart of Amos' God. True, Amos was made of stern stuff and was furious with the people for the evil in their midst, yet he did not wish disaster on them, rather he yearned and wept for their salvation. God's true servants have often been those of granite-like exterior, which hides a warm and passionate heart.

The third vision which he saw was of the Lord standing by a wall, which he was measuring. It had originally been built true to plumb, but was now in a perilous state. The plummet represented God's righteous standards, and measured by these Israel was a total disaster. This time Amos does not intercede. He knows it is too late, that the hand of divine judgment must fall. He hears the Lord say: *I will not change my mind again about punishing them ... I will bring the dynasty of king Jeroboam to an end* (7:8-9, GNB). Even so, he must have believed that there was still hope, for he went to Bethel to warn the Israelites there. In chapter 5 he graphically portrays Israel as a young virgin, in the prime of life, cut off by death, being carried in a funeral cortege. But the cortege pauses, the prophet preaches, and the hope is that the corpse will revive. But it was not to be. The cortege moves on. In a word, Amos saw the sword of Damocles hanging over the nation.

Anger and the Mind of God

Did Amos have a right to be angry? What was the cause of his anger? Does his anger truly represent the mind of God, as he believed? Or is it no more than personal irritation? Or is there some hidden motivation, which we must dig a little deeper to discover?

In the first place his anger rose out of his conception of who God is and what he expects of man, in particular of the chosen people, Israel. Perhaps we can best understand his conception of God by looking at those things which he considered made God angry. Basically they are three things: Idolatry, Immorality and Injustice. Let's look at each of these briefly.

Idolatry. This is the worship of images of gods. Man has always sought to conceptualise the divine in forms of art. This is dangerous because very often the worshipper ends up worshipping the art form in itself, perhaps often unconsciously. The Lord prohibited to Israel all forms of the use of images from the beginning. In the 10 Commandments, which were designed to form the 'Constitution' of the people of Israel, he states: *You shall not make for yourself an idol in the form of anything in heaven above or on the earth beneath or in the waters below. You shall not bow down to them or worship them* (Exod. 20:4-5). Strikingly, no image of the God of Israel has ever been discovered in any archaeological dig in modern Israel, though hundreds of pagan images have been discovered, and can be seen in museums in Israel, and in numerous outside Israel, today.

Immorality. Idolatry, immorality and injustice come together in the classic passage of Amos: *They (Israelites) trample on the heads of the poor... Father and son use the same girl and so profane my holy name. They lie down beside every altar on garments taken in pledge. In the house of their god they drink wine taken as fines* (2:7-8). Idolatry is spelt out in the references to 'the house of their god'. What is more startling to the modern reader is the reference to sexual activities being performed beside the altars in these temples.

As already stated in chapter 1, all ancient religions were fertility cults, in which sexual acts played a central role. This is mind blowing to the modern reader, in particular those who come from a Christian perspective. In the ancient world fertility of the land, of cattle, and of the human body were of enormous importance. You couldn't import wheat from distant lands, as we can today. If the harvest failed you were reduced to hunger, misery and death. If the calves and sheep did not produce young you were reduced to poverty. If you had no children, particularly male children, you had no guarantee of protection in the later years of life.

So you must have fertility at all cost, and ancient religions practised imitative magic in order to obtain these ends. The act of the devotee in sexual activity in the temple was believed to be seen by the gods, who would then themselves copulate in the heavens, which in turn would produce fertility on earth. Note the reference to drinking wine in the temple. Temples became centres of orgiastic feasts, with the wine flowing freely, and the climax came with the man indulging in sex with the prostitutes, paid and sustained by the temple. There were even male prostitutes. Amos complains (it must always be remembered that when we say 'Amos complains...' it is really the Lord complaining through Amos) that *Father and son use the same girl.* All moral standards have gone out the window in the rush for self-indulgence. Sex at any cost – which seems very much like a modern theme!

Ancient Israel turned in disgust from this gross sensuality, and her finer elements believed that it provoked the anger of the true God.

Injustice. In order to maintain a lifestyle built around continual feasting and sexual indulgence it became necessary for the rich and the powerful to exploit the poor. Thus they *trample on the heads of the poor* and *drink wine taken as fines.* This exploitation of the poor is one of Amos' major themes. We shall not explore it here, but return to it under the chapter on sociology.

It may be said that false religion, gross immorality, and exploitation of one's fellow men are bedfellows. False religion, which includes no religion, opens the door to immorality, and immorality becomes self-indulgence and greed, which eventually has to sustain itself by exploitation of others in society. Though Amos does not develop this theme, other prophets, like Isaiah and Micah, show that this then leads to a breakdown of society, to antagonisms, hatred, violence, and even civil war. It may well be that modern Western society is three quarters of the way along this road.

Amos' Conception of God

This is all important, for his idea of who God is, his likes and dislikes, his reaction to evil, are the basis of all Amos' attitudes and messages. Yet it must be remembered that Amos did not derive these entirely from his own notions. He inherited the faith of the true Israel. As a prophet he was not an innovator, but one who trod the ancient path marked out by Moses.

This dependence on the past is seen in the way in which he uses divine names. He uses a variety of combinations of names for God, which suggests he has given much thought to it. He speaks of God as: *'the LORD', 'the Sovereign LORD', 'the LORD Almighty', 'the Lord, the LORD Almighty', 'the LORD God Almighty', 'the Lord, the LORD God Almighty', 'the LORD your God', 'the LORD, whose name is God Almighty'.* Wow! This is all a bit much. We shall need to look at these more closely.

1. 'The LORD', in Hebrew, 'Yahweh' – 1:2 and throughout Amos' book. Note how the New International Version gives this in small capital letters, LORD. The translators say in the Preface: 'In regard to the divine name YHWH,... the translators adopted the device used in most English versions of rendering that name as 'LORD' in capital letters to distinguish it from Adonai, another Hebrew word rendered 'Lord', for which small letters are used.' One can see the difference clearly in Psalm 110:1: *The LORD said to my Lord, 'Sit at my right hand...'*, 'Yahweh said to my Adonai'.

The name Yahweh is extremely important in the Old Testament. It is not a title, as the translation 'Lord' might suggest, but rather a particular name of the God who revealed himself to Moses and the Israelites at the Exodus. It is the name of the One God who has linked himself in covenant with Israel at Mt. Sinai (Exod. 19-24). When Moses asked God about his Name, he replied: *Say to the Israelites, 'The LORD (Yahweh), the God of your fathers ... has sent me to you.' This is my name for ever, the name by which I am to be remembered from generation to generation* (Exod. 3:15). So Amos knows Yahweh as the God of covenant, of grace, of promise.

2. 'The Sovereign LORD'. See 1:8 (end) and frequently in Amos. The Hebrew text here joins the two names *YHWH* and *Adonai* together as a compound name of God, so our translators regard the latter as a description of the former. It means that Yahweh the God of Israel is in truth the Lord of all, of heaven and earth, of all that is. Surely a daring faith for such an apparently insignificant people.

3. 'The LORD Almighty', appears in Amos with many subtle combinations: 'the Lord, the LORD Almighty', 'the LORD God Almighty' (4:13); 'the Lord, the LORD God Almighty' (3:13; 5:16); 'the LORD, whose name is God Almighty'. The frequency of these phrases and the many variations Amos uses, give a great force to his use of them. So important are they that Amos is able to say, 'the LORD God Almighty is his name' (4:13). This he says, in effect, is the most complete name of God, the expression of his very being. What does it mean?

The basic phrase is *Yahweh zebaoth*, 'the LORD Almighty', which is translated in the older versions more literally as 'Lord of hosts' or as we might say today 'Lord of the Armies'. It seems to have been first used in Israel during the times of Samuel, Saul and David. An excellent example of its meaning at that time is found in the encounter of David with Goliath. David affirms: *You come against me with sword and spear and javelin, but I come against you in the name of the Lord Almighty (Yahweh zebaoth), the God of the armies of Israel, whom you have defied* (1 Sam. 17:45). David sees the Lord as standing at the head of Israel's army, guaranteeing its victory. Hundreds of years earlier, on the eve of his destruction of Jericho, Joshua learned that the Lord himself is *the commander of the Lord's army* (Josh. 5:15).

In many passages of the Old Testament the phrase appears in contexts in which the emphasis lies on the Lord's raising up an army, a foreign army, which is to fulfil some purpose of his. Thus in Isaiah 13:4 the Lord is seen as *The Lord Almighty [who] is mustering his army for war.* The army is not identified immediately. It seems to be a heavenly army, through which Yahweh *will punish the world for its evil,* but when the army emerges into the light of day it is the army of the Medes, who are attacking and destroying the Babylonian kingdom (v. 17). Perhaps there is a double meaning here. Behind every human power which is accomplishing the Lord's will stands the heavenly army, led by Yahweh of the Armies, dispatched to give his chosen human army the victory.

In another place, Isaiah 6:3, it is clearly the heavenly cohorts which he commands. The good king Uzziah, whom Isaiah knew and admired, had died. Israel was at the crossroads, with disaster looming. In the temple Isaiah saw *the Lord seated on a throne, high and exalted, and the train of his robe filled the temple...* Then the angelic voices sang,

"*Holy, holy, holy is the Lord Almighty;*
the whole earth is full of his glory."

Here clearly he heads the angelic armies, by which token he governs the destinies of all beings, earthly or heavenly.

We may summarise by saying that the title 'Lord Almighty' points to the fact that the God whom Amos worshipped was seen to be sovereign in power, whether over the armies of Israel, the powers that threatened her existence, or the powers that lie behind all human powers, that is angelic, or even demonic. We might compare this with Paul's affirmation that God *placed all things under Jesus' feet and appointed him to be head over everything for* (the benefit of) *the church* (Eph. 1:22).

The Loving Action of God

Central to all Old Testament thinking is the extraordinary goodness and kindness of the God who has revealed himself to Israel. We shall develop this later, but for the moment let us see how this worked itself out in the case of the chosen people according to Amos.

Election and Covenant. Though Amos does not use these words he uses similar concepts. At 2:10 God affirms that, *I brought you up out of Egypt, and I led you for forty years in the desert to give you the land of the Amorites.* This theme, normally termed the 'Exodus', lies at the very heart of all that Israel believed about their relationship to God. We have already looked at this in our chapter on history, so let me remind you of something we noted there:

For hundreds of years after this these realities will be inscribed in the very heart of everything Israel does in her finer moments. She sang about them in her songs, wrote them into her histories, celebrated them in her feasts. We find Amos, along with all the other prophets, using them as the yardstick by which to measure the people's faithfulness or unfaithfulness to the Lord.

Most important is the statement: *You only have I chosen of all the families of the earth; therefore I will punish you for all your sins* (3:2). Our modern translations obscure the fact that the word translated 'chosen' means more literally 'know' in Hebrew. 'Knowledge' in biblical language is more than mental understanding, it is the ability to enter into intimate relationship. Thus the literal translation of Genesis 4:1 is *Adam knew Eve, and she conceived and gave birth,* which the NIV translates freely,

Adam lay with his wife Eve... In other words, the verb is used for
the most intimate of all human relationships. So Israel was the
only nation with which the Lord had entered into intimate
relationship.

However, Amos is not using this to applaud Israel, or to lull
them into a false sense of security. Quite the opposite. Being God's
people required accepting the challenge to live as such, to be the
Lord's representatives, living a sweet and beautiful life, among
nations noted universally for their gross immorality, idolatry and
injustice. No other nation ever conceived of itself as entering into
an alliance with their God, much less one that had an essential
moral content.

At 2:4-5 Amos blasts his own country, Judah, *Because they
have rejected the law of the Lord and have not kept his decrees.*
Other nations have been condemned because of great cruelty
toward other peoples. Judah is condemned for disobedience to
the express will of God spelled out in the law. 'Law' in Hebrew is
Torah, to this day a very important word in all Jewish thought.
The word means something more than our concept of law as being
legal procedure. It would be better translated 'instruction' or
'teaching'. It is so translated in the book of Proverbs: *Listen, my
son, to your father's instruction and do not forsake your mother's
teaching...* (Prov. 1:8). It will be obvious that a mother's teaching
bears little resemblance to law in our modern usage. The point
here is that Yahweh had given to Israel instructions as to how to
conduct themselves as the chosen people, in order to be an example
to the nations of the good life.

Yet the language of law is also present in *Torah.* This is
evidenced by the strong use of legal terminology in the Old
Testament. God is a righteous judge, who observes the ways of
his people, rewarding them for obeying his commands, and
punishing them when they give themselves over to evil. This reality
was spelt out in the blessings and curses of the covenant. See
especially Deuteronomy 28, where obedience will lead to blessing:

You will be blessed in the city and blessed in the country. The
fruit of your womb will be blessed, and the crops of your land
and the young of your livestock ... Your basket and your
kneading trough will be blessed. You will be blessed when
you come in and blessed when you go out (28:1-17).

But disobedience will lead to the curses of the covenant (Deut.
28:18-68). These 51 verses contain terrible descriptions of
suffering which will come upon the people of the covenant. Being
chosen by God is not favouritism, but duty. Amos and his fellow
prophets barely needed divine revelation (though Amos had it in
his visions) to persuade them that disobedience would lead to
disaster, for it was written large in the terms of the special alliance
(covenant) which the Lord had offered to Israel. Indeed, when
Israel entered the land, they smashed their way through Jericho,
Bethel and Ai, in order to reach the town of Shechem, where, on
the twin peaks of Mts. Ebal and Gerizim, they pronounced the
blessings and curses of the covenant:

Cursed is the man who carves an image...
Cursed is the man who dishonours his father or his mother...
Cursed is the man who moves his neighbour's boundary stone...
Cursed is the man who leads the blind astray on the road...
Cursed is the man who withholds justice from the alien, the
fatherless or the widow...

and so on, for a total of 12 curses, after each of which ...'all the
people shall say, "Amen".' That is to say, they called the curses
down on their own heads.

Repentance was always an option for the prophets. Chapter 4 is
dedicated to the refusal of Israel to repent. 5:1-2 graphically
portrays Israel as a virgin, cut off in the prime of life, and glimpses
the funeral cortege. The procession is interrupted in verse 4 with
an extended invitation to Israel for a last-minute opportunity for

repentance, but there was no response, and the cortege resumes its deadly procession in verses 16-17.

150 years after Amos, the prophet Jeremiah found himself in a similar situation. As the army of the Babylonians ravaged the land, Jeremiah warned King Zedekiah:

> 'Hear the word of the LORD, O king of Judah .... Do what is just and right. Rescue from the hand of his oppressor the one who has been robbed. Do no wrong or violence to the alien, the fatherless, or the widow, and do not shed innocent blood in this place. For if you are careful to carry out these commands, then kings who sit on David's throne will come through the gates of this palace, riding in chariots and on horses .... But if you do not obey these commands .... I swear by myself that this palace will become a ruin' (Jer. 22:2-5).

God's Anger. The failure of the call to repentance leads to the certainty of divine judgment: *I will crush you .... An enemy will overrun the land; he will pull down your strongholds and plunder your fortresses .... I will send you into exile beyond Damascus* (2:13; 3:11; 5:27). If you have read the book of Amos, as you were urged to do in the Introduction, you will recognise that there are many similar passages in his book.

Notice that this judgment is divinely personal, '*I* will crush you....' It is not merely impersonal forces, but the presence of the living God within and through these forces, material and political, which achieves the objective of the destruction of Israel.

Are Anger and Love incompatible? There is a tendency today to paint God's attitude to us as all sweet and light. The idea of God's being angry would even be seen by some as offensive. A word of caution first. Most human anger is fitful and tainted with human sin. Divine anger is never so. It is an overflowing of the negative reacting of God against all evil. We need now to ask ourselves whether anger and mercy are compatible with each other.

There is an idea abroad that there is an inherent contradiction between the Old Testament and the New. The Old, it is thought, paints a grim picture of the anger and wrath of God against human sin, whilst the basic theme of the New is that God is loving, kind and merciful. I want to suggest that this is far from the truth. Some of the hardest words about divine anger and judgment are found in the New Testament, and often in the words of Jesus. But I will point to two solid facts from the Old Testament which undermine the idea.

First, there is the worship chant, the central worship chant, of the Old Testament:

> **'give thanks to the Lord,**
> **for he is good, his love endures for ever.'**

Psalm 136 is clearly meant as a responsive chant. As the priest cried: *O give thanks to the Lord, for he is good,* the people responded: *His love endures for ever.* The priest cried: *Give thanks to the God of gods,* and the people replied again, *His love endures for ever.* The priest exhorted, *Give thanks to the Lord of Lords,* and the people responded with one voice, *His love endures for ever.* Read the psalm, with its 26 affirmations about the goodness of God, with the responsive chant, *His love endures for ever.*

Psalm 118 begins with this same exclamation, probably made by the priest, who then turned to the congregation, saying, *Let Israel say...* and the mass of the people chanted back, *His love endures for ever;* he then said, *Let the house of Aaron say...,* and the priests chanted, *His love endures for ever;* He then intoned, *Let those who fear the Lord say:...* and the whole congregation, priests and people responded, *His love endures for ever.* The psalm concludes with the great cry.

Other psalms begin with this chant, and then launch into a description of areas in which the Lord's extraordinary love has been demonstrated. So Psalm 106, which gives a lengthy account of the utter unfaithfulness of the Israelites, begins by affirming this basic theology that the Lord is utterly good, His love endures for ever. Psalm 107 is dedicated to those sufferers all over the world who had called on the name of the Lord, and found support from him, and is prefaced by this same cry: *Give thanks to the LORD for he is good, his love endures for ever.*

Apparently the cry was an essential part of Israel's worship. A psalm said to have been given by David to the temple choir (1 Chron. 16:34) at the very beginning of the times of Israelite worship, draws toward its conclusion with this very same acclamation. Again, David's son, Solomon, is shown giving instructions to the worship leaders at the inauguration of the Temple in Jerusalem:

> They were accompanied by 120 priests sounding trumpets. The trumpeters and singers joined in unison, as with one voice, to give praise and thanks to the LORD. Accompanied by trumpets, cymbals and other instruments, they raised their voices in praise to the LORD and sang: 'He is good, his love endures for ever' (2 Chron. 5:12-13).

No doubt they sang more than this, much more, but this was the essence of everything they sang. Finally we hear the same note sounded as King Jehoshaphat led his people into battle:

> Jehoshaphat appointed men to sing to the LORD and to praise him for the splendour of his holiness as they went out at the head of the army, saying: 'Give thanks to the LORD, for his love endures for ever' (2 Chron. 20:21).

What shall we conclude from all this? Here was a people whose worship and thought were soaked in the belief in the essential goodness and love of God.

Second, we must pass on to another piece of convincing evidence
that Amos' God was thoroughly loving. Very early in the history
of the nation, Moses had asked the Lord: 'Now show me your
glory' (Exod. 33:18), and the Lord responded by hiding Moses in
a rock and passing by him, and as he did so, he proclaimed his
Name:

> **The LORD, the LORD,**
> **the compassionate and gracious God,**
> **slow to anger,**
> **abounding in love and faithfulness,**
> **maintaining love to thousands,**
> **and forgiving wickedness,**
> **rebellion and sin**
>
> Exodus 34:6

This is the most important, the most fundamental statement about
God in the Old Testament. Much could be said in unpacking this
statement, but space does not permit. Read it over several times
and ask yourself what every clause means.

Now at first glance we might regard this as yet another general
statement about God, were it not for the fact that this affirmation
considerably expands on the previous one we looked at, and we
soon discover that this statement was repeated and echoed
numerous times in the Old Testament, and always in very special
circumstances. I have before me no less than 12 passages in which
it is quoted, but I shall point to only four.

First, when the Israelites had flagrantly committed evil, and
the Lord threatened to destroy them, Moses reminded the Lord of
his own statement: '...just as you have declared: 'The LORD is
slow to anger, abounding in love and forgiving sin and rebellion....''
In accordance with your great love, forgive the sin of these
people...' (Num. 14:17-19). Through citing the Lord's own words
back at him, Moses claimed forgiveness for his people. It seems

almost an impertinence for him to speak to God in this way, but
Moses knew he had every right to remind God of his own character.

Given the fact that echoes of it are found many times in the
Psalms (see 86:5, 15; 103:8; 111:4; 112:4; 116:5; 145:8), it is not
surprising that the minds of the Israelites are soaked in this
sentiment. When Jonah was sent to Nineveh to preach the coming
doom of that city, he did a runner and escaped to foreign parts.
Thrown into the sea and swallowed by a large fish, he is saved by
the graciousness of God and dispatched anew on his God-
appointed task. 'Yet 40 days and Nineveh will perish' was his cry
as he preached in that city. Nineveh repented of its evil, and the
Lord forgave their sin.

Nineveh did not perish. Jonah, however, was not well pleased
with this. In fact he 'became angry', and complained to the Lord:
'Is this not what I said when I was still at home? That is why I
was so quick to flee to Tarshish. I knew that you are a gracious
God, slow to anger and abounding in love, a God who relents
from sending calamity' (Jonah 4:2). Jonah the nationalist had no
wish for Nineveh, the hated enemy of his people, to repent and be
saved from God's wrath, and this is the reason why he did a bunk.
He knew that love and compassion were the basic traits of God's
character, that his righteous anger is 'his strange work ... his alien
task' (Isa. 28:21). From the beginning he had known that the
slightest sign of remorse would get Nineveh off the hook, such
was the love and kindness of his God.

Our final example is from Micah, who prophesied in Judah
within a generation of the preaching of Amos. Micah, like Amos,
lashes out furiously at the rich and powerful who exploit the poor
and the weak. Like Amos he expects the unleashing of the anger
of God in destructive judgment upon the nation. Yet as he draws
to a close, he asks: 'Who is a God like you, who pardons sin and
forgives the transgression of the remnant of his inheritance? You
do not stay angry for ever but delight to show mercy. You will
again have compassion on us; you will tread our sins underfoot
and hurl all our iniquities into the depths of the sea' (7:18-19).

Every year at Yom Kippur, the biblical Day of Atonement, Jews in their synagogues world-wide recite these words.

However, I must add in one other element, for I cut short the quotation in Exodus 34:6, and we must now hear the rest of the divine character: '... *forgiving wickedness, rebellion and sin. Yet he does not leave the guilty unpunished ....*' The biblical writers, whilst inheriting the faith of their fathers that the Lord is essentially gracious, loving and forgiving, never lost sight of the fact that God punishes evil. God does not mollycoddle us. He is not a benevolent grandfather, patting us affectionately on the head whenever we do wrong. From the very nature of his being he reacts negatively towards evil. If he did not do so he would not be God, and would not be worthy of our worship. In a very real sense the prophets did not need special divine revelation for them to understand that God would punish Israel for its sin, it was written large in the terms of the covenant relationship that God had given them.

We may summarise by saying that Israel's faith was grounded in the belief that Yahweh their God was the only God, the only ultimate power in the universe; that his character was marked by undying love and compassion; and that he reacted in anger whenever and wherever he saw idolatry, immorality and injustice.

Religion, the true and the false

Our title is not a sectarian slogan. Religious practices are a visible expression of the beliefs, the faith, the theology of the worshippers. Amos and his fellow-prophets were convinced that Israel's religious practices were either tainted with paganism or insincere, or both. It is not easy to judge the degree of paganism which is being attacked, nor of hypocrisy as the people went about their religious worship. Though the northerners had built alternative temples at Bethel and Dan, it was never their intention to abandon the worship of Yahweh.

Most likely the religion of Israel at this time was one of syncretism, which is the blending of the worship of Yahweh with that of pagan forms, thus corrupting the former. Elijah saw this clearly when he accused Israel of 'wavering between two opinions' (1 Kings 18:21). For Elijah, fusing the worship of Yahweh with that of Baal was simply not on. To many moderns this sounds more like religious bigotry. Why not mix the two? Why this exclusiveness of the worship of Yahweh?

The basic elements of Baalism

The fact is that the true Israelite saw the worship of Baal as the moral and spiritual pits. In an important passage in Isaiah 57:3-9, the prophet brings together various elements which made Baalism repugnant to the Israelites.

> Come here to be judged, you sinners! You are no better than sorcerers, adulterers, and prostitutes .... You worship the fertility gods by having sex under those sacred trees of yours. You offer your children as sacrifices in the rocky caves near the bed of a stream .... You set up your obscene idols just inside your front doors. You forsake me; you take off your clothes and climb into your large beds with your lovers .... And there you satisfy your lusts (GNB).

We can here identify various elements of Canaanite religion.

1. Idolatry. Idolatry is the act of posturing in worship before figures representing the divine. In an earlier passage, 44:9-20, idolatry is satirised as the height of absurdity and crass stupidity. Isaiah points out that they take a log of wood, use part of it for making a fire to warm themselves with, another part they use for cooking bread, and then use the rest to create an image, before which they prostrate themselves: 'No-one stops to think, no-one has the knowledge or understanding to say, "Half of it I used for fuel; I even baked bread over its coals, I roasted meat and I ate. Shall I make a detestable thing from what is left? Shall I bow down to a block of wood?" ' (verse 19). The whole passage has to be read in order to feel the full weight of this ridicule.

To us this may seem all very simple, but in a world where no-one ever conceived of worshipping gods except in some physical form of representation, the rejection by true Israelites of every form of idol worship was revolutionary.

2. Sexual orgies. This is what Amos is referring to when he first blasts off against Israel: *Father and son use the same girl and so profane my holy name.* This girl was either a slave girl, or more likely a temple prostitute. We have already referred above to these orgies, which were practised in the temple. Isaiah 57 vividly accuses them of lust. Oaks and spreading trees were often considered sacred to the inhabitants of a sun-baked land, where the shade provided by trees was enormously important, so that they came to be regarded as sacred. Away from the temples these became the next best thing for the practice of adultery and fornication.

Male prostitutes, no doubt for homosexual acts, were also provided in the native religion of Baalism. Solemnly the biblical historian paints the Sodomism that came to be attractive to many in Judah as the nation hit the pits: 'There were even male shrine-prostitutes in the land, the people engaged in all the detestable practices of the nations the LORD had driven out before the Israelites' (1 Kings 14:24). At its lowest disgusting point, special quarters were built to house the male shrine-prostitutes in the Lord's temple in Jerusalem (2 Kings 23:7).

3. Child Sacrifice. Isaiah 57 goes on to say, significantly in the same sentence in which he points to their sexual orgies: '...you sacrifice your children in the ravines and under the overhanging crags'. In the ancient Near East remains of children, who had been sacrificed, have been found, from birth to 17 years of age. The nation most renowned for this was the Phoenicians, where Baalism reigned supreme as the state religion, and it was the Phoenician type of Baalism which threatened Israel's worship of the Lord.

Two kings of Judah, Ahaz and Manasseh, offered their first-born sons to the god Molech. It is probable that it was primarily in moments of great danger that these sacrifices were offered, and it also seems to have had a cruel attraction to those who held the reigns of power. It was a way of pacifying the anger of the god, perceived in the danger which threatened. We have a graphic picture of one such occasion in 2 Kings 3:26-27: 'When the king of Moab saw that the battle had gone against him, he took with him 700 swordsmen to break through to the king of Edom, but they failed. Then he took his firstborn son, who was to succeed him as king, and offered him as a sacrifice on the city wall.' One can imagine this scene. As the horrified Israelites watched from below, the king solemnly offered up his son, to the sound of music and trumpets. But it had the desired effect, and the Israelites lifted the siege and returned to their land.

Ancient writers tell us of the special role of music on such occasions. It was played at the highest possible pitch in order that the parents of the child might not hear its screams. Do you not now see why Baalism could never be grafted on to the worship of Yahweh?

This horrific act was performed frequently in the latter years of Israel just outside the walls of Jerusalem, in the valley of Ben Hinnom, which lay to the south of the city. Today, the top of the valley is a delightful park, and one descends it through olive groves to emerge on a dusty football pitch where Arab boys kick a football. It is hard to imagine the utter horror of child sacrifice in such a tranquil setting today.

When the final curtain closed on the children of Israel in the land of promise, as the armies of Babylon closed in on Jerusalem, the prophet Jeremiah had no doubt that it was primarily because of this abomination that the Lord destroyed the nation: 'The people of Israel have done evil in my eyes .... They have built the high places .... in the Valley of Ben Hinnom to burn their sons and daughters in the fire – something I did not command nor did it enter my mind' (Jer. 7:30, 31).

A people who spent their times in sexual orgies, with the official blessing of the religious system, would never be content with ordinary ways of living, and to maintain their orgiastic feasts they resorted to the exploitation of others. But more of that in a later chapter. Suffice to say that it led to the disintegration of society.

Religion versus the truth

Religion can be an enemy to the truth. In spite of the grave dangers of Baalism, it is not evident that all the people of Israel were steeped in it. Indeed this is not Amos' accusation. He is quite clear that there is a lot of religion going on in the country, and that it professes to be a worship of Yahweh, the God of Israel. But religion had become divorced from the truth, from godliness, from justice and righteousness. At best it was a shallow imitation of true worship, and therefore hypocritical.

Amos mentions several places which had become centres of worship to which the people flocked. These places often had holy associations with the history of the people. In 5:4-6 he mentions Bethel, Gilgal and Beersheba. So far from considering that 'holy places' had a unique significance, Amos sees that when such worship is divorced from truth it is ripe for divine judgment: *Gilgal will surely go into exile, and Bethel will be reduced to nothing* (5:5), *the sanctuaries of Israel will be ruined* (7:9).

A few years later Isaiah (Isa. 1:10-17) returned to the same theme, blasting the worship practised in the temple of Yahweh in Jerusalem. He pictures the people trampling the temple courts like dumb animals. The sacrificial system, which the Lord himself had ordered, has become repugnant to him, their special feasts he detests, and even their prayers descend on his deaf ears. Why? Because they have become divorced from goodness of life. The only antidote to his anger is 'wash and make yourselves clean. Take your evil deeds out of my sight! Stop doing wrong, learn to do right! Seek justice, encourage the oppressed. Defend the cause of the fatherless, plead the case of the widow.' All the prophets echo this same theme, but space limits us.

Suffice to return to Amos. *'I hate, I despise your religious feasts; I cannot stand your assemblies …. Away with the noise of your songs! I will not listen to the music of your harps.'* What then does the Lord want? *'Let justice roll on like a river, righteousness like a never-failing stream!'* (5:21-24).

Amos looked at the religion of Israel, whether the paganized religion or the merely formal, hypocritical religion of the apparently orthodox, and saw it as an enemy of the truth. For the truth cannot be merely formal. It must be passionate, it must be whole-blooded. Truth requires total devotion of the one who professes to hold it. Amos the thinker sees the dangers of a half-hearted devotion to truth. It leads to compromise, and compromise leads to permissiveness, and permissiveness to moral corruption, and moral corruption to exploitation of others, and to the ultimate disintegration of society.

The Religion of Israel

The people of Israel knew that their faith, in its outward apparatus of religion, had been ordered by the Lord at Sinai (Exod. 25-40), and was an integral part of the covenant. It had numerous parts.

The Temple. Initially the tabernacle, and then the temple in Jerusalem which Solomon built, was the central focus of Israelite faith. The love of the temple is echoed in several psalms (see 48, 63, 84), and at its purest it contributed to the life of the people. It was designed to be a symbol of the presence of God among his people.

Priesthood. Full details are given for the clothes of the priests (Exod. 28), which by their magnificence distinguished them in their appearance. The magnificence of the temple combined with the attire of the priests to give a vivid sense of the glory of God. The priesthood was limited to the descendants of the first high priest, Aaron.

Levites. In a sense these were a second level of priesthood, yet they could never pass to the top level. Their responsibility was to serve the priesthood and the temple. Some will have done this as a sacred privilege: 'I would rather be a doorkeeper in the house of my God ...' (Psalm 84:10), but the fact that Ezra found that Levites were very unwilling to return from the Exile (Ezra 8:15-20) suggests that they did not always enjoy this role.

Sacrifices. A complicated system of sacrifices of animals to Yahweh was established. Basically there were five types: sin and guilt offerings, whole burnt offerings, grain offerings, and fellowship offerings. The first two were expressions of repentance for sins committed. The whole burnt offering was totally consumed in the flames, with the offerer laying his hands on the animal as an expression of his total surrender to the will of God.

Fellowship offerings were the most commonly practised, and were subdivided into three types: the 'expression of thankfulness' (Lev. 7:12), the fulfilment of a vow, and the freewill offering, which was what one offered simply because you wanted to. The grain offering is the only one in which blood was not shed, yet it never seems to have been offered alone, but always alongside blood offerings.

More could be said about the Sabbath and the Feasts of Israel, but space does not permit. What did it all mean? All of these, whilst having an immediate message for the Israelite, pointed beyond themselves. God was in the business of audio-visuals long before the modern age.

The temple, symbol of the presence of God among his people, pointed forward to the earthly presence of Jesus, the Son of God. Speaking of his earthy body, he could say: 'Destroy this temple, and I will raise it again in three days...' But the temple he had spoken of was his body (John 2:19-21). The priesthood pointed forward to Jesus as our great high priest, who has entered into our sorrows, and has offered up the only perfect sacrifice for sin, whilst the blood character of the whole sacrificial system pointed forward to the one offering which Jesus made for our sin at Calvary.

Temple, priesthood and sacrificial system came under the lash of the prophets' rebukes. Jeremiah stood at the gate of the temple and shouted to the people going in: 'Do not trust in deceptive words and say, "This is the temple of the LORD, the temple of the LORD, the temple of the LORD" ' (7:4). Parroting religious trite words will not do, only a moral transformation would be acceptable. The priests and Levites became corrupt time-servers of the rich and the powerful, whilst the sacrificial system came to be used as a way of buying God's favour (Amos 5:21-24).

The antidote to this corruption of the system is wonderfully expressed by Isaiah: 'This is the one I esteem: he who is humble and contrite in spirit, and trembles at my word' (66:2). If that does not accompany the divinely appointed system, Isaiah says, then that in itself becomes totally repugnant to God, and indeed sinful (66:3).

Jesus and Amos

Amos would have concurred heartily with an affirmation of Jesus: 'If you hold to my teaching, you are really my disciples. Then you will know the truth, and the truth will set you free' (John 8:31-32). For the prophets the 'teachings' were conserved in the law which the Lord had given to Israel at Sinai (Jer. 11:1-8). Only by pledging oneself to that law (real disciples to its demands) could one know the truth, and only thus could freedom be found. The law of God was not and is not a yoke around our necks, but the truest experience of freedom. There are four elements in this search for true freedom, like links in a chain (see next page).

The end process which human society requires is *freedom* for every person. Jesus says that freedom is not a state in itself, but the product of other forces. These begin with his teaching, which it is necessary to hold on to. Like Israel's law, the teachings of Jesus are not there for our curiosity. They require commitment on part of the one who hears them, commitment to a way of life which marks one out as a disciple of Jesus. It is such a

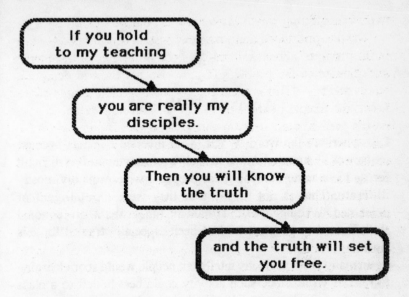

If you hold
to my teaching

you are really my
disciples.

Then you will know
the truth

and the truth will set
you free.

wholehearted acceptance of the teaching and way of life of Jesus which leads us to the truth, and the truth to freedom.

The Right Way of Thinking

The Old Testament thinkers always leave us with a feeling that more needs to be said. Amos and his fellow-prophets raised fundamental questions about the nature of truth and a person's commitment to it. For them truth was centred in the law of Yahweh, the God of Israel, the only true God. Jesus takes up these scattered threads of Old Testament thinking and teaching. In themselves they are the beginnings of divine revelation, raising questions, but always leaving us with the feeling that much more remains to be said. In the teachings of Jesus they find their true fulfilment, for righteousness, which for the prophets was an elusive ideal, becomes a reality in Jesus Christ, the Son of God. He has perfected truth and brought it to us from the heart of the Father (John 1:18).

5

Amos the 'Writer'

I have written the word 'writer' with inverted commas because
we cannot be sure that Amos himself wrote anything! It is difficult
for us to imagine that the great prophets were probably mostly
illiterate. That is not to say that they were unintelligent or
unlearned. Writing in Old Testament times was a professional
skill, limited to people who had been especially trained for this
work.

In many cases perfectly intelligent people would scorn learning
to read or write, since such activity could best be left to a class
below them. Today we tend to think that only ignorant people are
unable to read and write. This at least ought to be a warning to us
against such arrogance.

What do we know about writing in ancient times?

How soon would the books of the Old Testament, and especially
those by prophets, have been written down? The one certain
evidence of prophetical gift was the fulfilment of prophecy. In
Jerusalem, where Amos' oracles will have been known and talked
about, an earthquake within two years of his preaching must have
sent shock waves through the city, and projected his prophecies
onto 'front page' news. Amos had prophesied just such an event
(1:2; 8:8; 9:5), and now the whole country had been rocked by an
earthquake, which was to be remembered for more than 200 years.
In Zechariah 14:5 we have a glimpse of panic-stricken people
fleeing from the earthquake.

It is reasonable to assume that someone would have made sure
that his prophecies were written down very soon after. Did the
prophet personally direct the project? Did he employ a personal

108

scribe, or was it undertaken with his collaboration by those who admired him? We know that both of these possibilities were used by later prophets. Within 20-25 years of Amos, Isaiah instructed his followers, his disciples, to put his early prophecies into writing (Isa. 8:16), at a time when he apparently withdrew from public ministry. No doubt he would have had a very large part in controlling what was put into the scroll.

On the other hand, more than a century after Amos, we find Jeremiah employing a personal secretary (scribe): *So Jeremiah called Baruch son of Neriah, and while Jeremiah dictated all the words the LORD had spoken to him, Baruch wrote them on the scroll* (Jer. 36:4). He then instructed Baruch to read them aloud to the people gathered in the temple, since he himself was forbidden to go there. There need be little doubt that Amos could have used one of these methods.

Poetry. The first formal thing that strikes us about the writings of the prophets is that they are written in *poetic* form. Since Hebrew poetry differs strikingly from our modern forms, the way to detect poetry in a modern translation is that the translators have given us short lines for poetry, and long, unbroken lines, for prose. Thus Amos 1:1 is a prose title for the book, whilst verse 2 is immediately poetic and this poetry is maintained almost unbroken until we reach chapter 7. Since this chapter is mainly a description of Amos' vision and of his clash with Amaziah, the priest of Bethel, it is written in prose. Yet even here, wherever Amos' message, or God's message through him, comes into play, it is written in poetic form (e.g. vv. 9, 11, 17).

Why did the prophets use poetic form? Probably in the first place because poetry was far more widespread then than today. It was a vital form of communication. In fact we know that the first history books, in the world of the early prophets, were written in poetic form. In Numbers 21:14-15 a poetic passage is cited from a book called 'The Book of the Wars of the LORD'. Perhaps this was Israel's first history book, which is quoted in order to establish a point about geographic locations relating to boundary disputes. Later in the same chapter a larger passage is quoted with the introduction, 'That is why the poets say...' (verse 27), and the poetry quoted describes a pre-Israelite war among the local inhabitants of the land. One can catch a feeling of the poet standing among the seated clans, describing tales of the conflicts of the peoples of the land. Poets were probably responsible for conserving the early history of the people.

There was a time when some argued that Moses could not possibly have written any part of the early books of the Bible because writing was not known then. We now know that writing began about 2,000 years before Moses, which means something like 2,500 years before Amos, around 3,200 BC. By the time Moses arrived in the promised land, the Phoenicians (i.e. Canaanites) had developed a functional alphabet.

But the poetry was not the work of scribes, who were probably quite dull fellows, slavishly copying what was dictated to them. Rather, the prophets themselves seem to have had the habit of putting their thoughts, which they knew to be divinely inspired, into poetic form. The poetic form will have enabled them, and their followers, to remember more easily the content of their messages.

Amos 1:2 is an excellent example of ancient Hebrew poetry.

The LORD roars from Zion
    and thunders from Jerusalem;
the pastures of the shepherds dry up,
    and the top of Carmel withers.

You will notice that both of these sets of two lines are parallel to each other. Zion is the name of an area of the city of Jerusalem, which eventually came to be used poetically for the whole city. Also the two verbs, 'roar' and 'thunder', give the same impression of two frightening human experiences, the roar of the lion and the clap of thunder. In the second set the verbs, 'dry up' and 'wither', mean essentially the same thing, whilst 'Carmel' is noted for its 'pastures of the shepherds'. In other words, the second line

Canaan News

Technological Advance by our great Canaanite culture

Reports are coming into our office at Tyre that scientific linguists have achieved the first sub-system of cuneiform, called 'THE ALPHABET'.

We are no longer enslaved to time-wasting pictographic and syllabic cuneiform. In future we shall only need 30 letters for writing thousands of words.

Hurrah for Canaanite cultural advance!

Speaking to the media and diplomatic corps at Tyre, King Hiram declared this to be further evidence of his country's vast cultural superiority.

expresses a thought which is *parallel* in meaning to the first line, and the fourth expresses a thought parallel to the third. The lines stand parallel to each other. Scholars refer to this as 'parallelism'.

Parallelism is the most notable form of Hebrew poetry, and it is particularly good in the Psalms. Hebrew poetry is not dependent on rhyme or metre, but rather on

　　1. Rhythm of Sound – a regular pattern of accented syllables.
　　2. Rhythm of Thought – sense, or meaning, rhythm.

　　If it is asked how the biblical scholar can recognise poetry and distinguish it from prose, the answer is by means of the rhythm of sound, accompanied by rhythm of thought. It is quite impossible to reproduce the rhythm of sound in English, but fortunately the rhythm of thought or of meaning is translatable into any other language. The Christian will feel that this was due to the over-riding sovereignty of an all-wise God. This balanced rhythm of thought and clause is also found in other early cultures, but was polished and used to greatest effect in the Old Testament.

Psalm 51　Examples of simple, or synonymous parallelism:

2　*Wash away*	*all my iniquity*
cleanse me	*from my sin*
5　*Surely I was sinful*	*at birth*
sinful	*from the time my mother*
	conceived me
6　*Surely you desire truth*	*in the inner parts,*
you teach me wisdom	*in the inmost place.*
7　*Cleanse me with hissop*	*and I shall be clean*
wash me	*and I shall be whiter than snow.*

In each of these verses, the second line repeats the first in its precise order. We can put 'a' for the first phrase, and 'b' for the second, and represent it thus:

$$\left. \begin{matrix} a\text{-}b \\ a\text{-}b \end{matrix} \right\} \text{ type}$$

In contrast verses 3 and 4 interchange the phrases in the second line:

3 For I know	*my transgressions*
and my sin	*is always before me.*
4 Against you, you only	*have I sinned*
and done what is evil	*in your sight*

You will see that the 4th phrase of each couplet repeats the first, and the 3rd repeats the second. We can represent this thus:

$$\left. \begin{array}{l} a - b \\ b - a \end{array} \right\} \text{type}$$

Another type of parallelism, very characteristic of the Book of Proverbs, uses a contrasting or antithetical type of parallelism, where the second statement is intended to say the opposite to the first.

Whoever loves discipline loves knowledge,
but he who hates correction is stupid (Prov. 12:1).

A gentle answer turns away wrath,
but a harsh word stirs up anger (Prov. 15:1; cp. 10:1-7).

Antithetical parallelism is nearly always negative and is designed to shock the reader into reality. It rubs his nose into the harsh realities of life.

Of course Hebrew poetry is more complex than simple parallelism, but there is a constant tendency toward repetitive thought, which is by no means boring, and can be very stimulating. It is even felt in the New Testament, especially in some of the sayings of Jesus:

In the same way you judge others, you will be judged;
and with the measure you use, it will be measured to you

which is typical of the a - b, a - b type.

Matthew 7:7 *Ask, and it shall be given to you,*
seek, and you shall find,
knock, and it shall be opened to you.

In this latter example, it would be foolish to try to make a distinction between the three exhortations 'ask...seek...knock', for they are all ways of saying the same thing. This is sometimes called 'step' parallelism, as we seem to be climbing higher with each clause.

I once heard a preacher declaiming on the words of Jesus: 'You shall worship the Lord your God, and him only shall you serve' (Matt. 4:10). The essence of his message was that this proved that 'worship' and 'serve' were two quite distinct things. In reality it proves the contrary. If the two clauses are in parallel, then to serve is to worship, to worship is to serve. If the preacher had been aware of the simple rule of parallelism he would not have fallen into such an unfortunate mistake.

Vivid Imagery. If there is one thing which distinguishes poetry in any language from prose, it is vivid picture language. Poetry is full of picture language, and Amos' message is full of poetic imagery. A student of mine once interpreted the threshing sledge at Amos 1:3 as meaning that the Syrians laid Israelites out on the ground and ran threshing sledges over them! The dead hand of literalism has too often marred our interpretation of Scripture. In this way the Bible's defenders have too often done more damage than its detractors! There are also passages in prose in which the writer will wax enthusiastic and overflow with figurative language, but this is in reality a kind of poetic prose.

Consider for example this picture of God moving into action:

'The earth trembled and quaked,
and the foundations of the mountains shook;
they trembled because he was angry.
Smoke rose from his nostrils;

consuming fire came from his mouth,
    burning coals blazed out of it.
He parted the heavens and came down;
    dark clouds were under his feet...
Out of the brightness of his presence clouds advanced,
    with hailstones and bolts of lightning...' (Psalm 18:7-12).

You will appreciate that this is colourful language. What actually happened was that David found himself holed up behind a rock, whilst the soldiers of Saul moved in. His prayer went up to the Lord, and a messenger arrived to inform Saul that the Philistines were attacking his land. Saul withdrew his troops and David was saved (1 Sam. 23:19-28). The hymn celebrates that salvation in superlative language.

So vivid is the language of biblical poetry that even God may be pictured vividly. Thus in Amos 1:2 he is compared to the roaring lion terrorizing its prey, or to a clap of thunder. In Hosea the language is even more strikingly vivid: 'For I will be like a lion to Ephraim .... I will tear them to pieces and go away; I will carry them off, with no-one to rescue them' (5:14); he is like an infuriated bear whose cubs have been robbed, who rips open her opponents (13:8); he is like a moth buzzing around the people's head (5:12).

Biography is limited in Amos' book to 1:1 and 7:10-15. We have the scantiest knowledge of his life circumstances. He describes himself as *a shepherd, and I also took care of sycamore-fig trees.* We have already discussed the nature of his life in our chapter on culture, so will not repeat it here. He certainly had a head-on clash with the priest of the royal sanctuary at Bethel. But we must confess that other matters of his life can only be gleaned by hints here and there, for example, that his shepherd life must have been very similar to the rugged circumstances in which young David played out his shepherd role: 'Your servant has been keeping his father's sheep. When a lion or a bear came and carried off a sheep from the flock, I went after it and struck it and rescued the sheep from its mouth. When it turned on me, I seized it by its hair, struck it and killed it' (1 Sam. 17:34-36). Compare this with the description of Amos: *As a shepherd saves from the lion's mouth only two leg bones or a piece of an ear...* (3:12).

Of some prophets, such as Joel, we know absolutely nothing of their life's circumstances, yet of others, and in particular Jeremiah, we know a lot. We learn from his book that he was at an early time in his service put on trial for treason (Jer. 26), which would have carried the death sentence. The men of his home village of Anathoth, near Jerusalem, were so embarrassed by his preaching doom in the big city, that they tried to murder him (11:18-23). On another occasion he walked into an international conference in the city wearing a yoke around his neck in order to warn the ambassadorial delegates that it was no use fighting against Babylon. The best way was submission (chap. 27). He was imprisoned, at one point dumped down a cistern with mud at the bottom (chap. 38). At the end we find him as an exile in distant Egypt, preaching his heart out to his people there.

Yes, biography plays a large part in the Old Testament, and is one of its chief contributions to literature. Who has not been moved by the narrative of Joseph's slavery in Egypt; by the exploits of David, fleeing from Saul's cruel vindictiveness; by the tender sweetness of Ruth in the fields of Boaz; by Queen Esther's pleading for the salvation of her people?

Brevity is a note of excellence in biblical reporting. The writer can say a lot with a great economy of words. The three visions in Amos 7:1-9 are not discursive narratives, but are reduced to essentials and designed with a clear pattern. Very much more happened than what is recounted. His prayer, for example, *Sovereign LORD, forgive! How can Jacob survive? He is so small,* must surely be a brief synthesis of a much longer prayer in which he pleaded for the life of Israel.

Wisdom in Israel

Amos and the other prophets did not live their lives in a protective shell. They were very much involved in the day-to-day life of their people. We shall refer to various classes of people – royalty, officials, judges, priests, landowners, and others – in our chapter on sociology.

There is a type of person in Amos' time for which we have less detail, but they must have been important. Amos will have known of them, even if he did not rub shoulders with them in the village of Tekoa. We know them best as city people, part of the culture of the educated classes. They are the wise men, who seem to have lived mainly in the capital, Jerusalem. Though they do not appear in Amos' book they are mentioned several times in the works of those prophets who lived in Jerusalem – Isaiah and Jeremiah – to which we shall return later.

Though Amos may never have met a wise man, as part of the general culture his prophecies show influences of their writing styles. This serves to emphasize that the prophetic scriptures did not come down to us ready-made from heaven, but were hammered out on the anvil of real life.

Strangely, we know less about the wise men, even though they created the great literature of Proverbs, Ecclesiastes and Job, than we do about the prophets and priests. Jeremiah identifies these three types of people as representing influential forces in the nation, 'The teaching of the law by the *priest* will not be lost, nor will counsel from the *wise*, nor the word from the *prophets*' (18:18). Priests and prophets need little explanation, not so the wise.

Why do we know so little about them? I think because they had no historian to record their activities and further their cause. The books of Kings were clearly inspired within prophetic circles. The accounts of the ministries of Elijah and Elisha recorded in Kings give us a clear picture of the daily round and public ministry of the lives of the prophets. On the other hand the books of Chronicles record the history of Israel through the eyes of the priests, and give us many details of the lives, ministry, and even courage of the priests.

But no-one presented the history from the viewpoint of the wise. On the one hand this is surprising, since the wise men were particularly favoured by royalty, and also had easy access to all the forms of reading and writing. Yet on the other hand their writings show little or no interest in history.

Wisdom Schools in the ancient world

We know from several sources the activities of wise men in the ancient world, and the prophets themselves were knowledgeable of them. Jeremiah scornfully asks: 'Is there no longer wisdom in Teman? Has counsel perished from the prudent? Has their wisdom decayed?' (Jer. 49:7).We note the attribution of wisdom, counsel and prud-ence to certain people. Interestingly, the tiny land of Edom seems to have been notable as a centre for wisdom (Obad. 8).

Egypt was particularly renowned for its wisdom schools. Isaiah ridicules these: 'The officials of Zoan are nothing but fools; the wise counsellors of Pharaoh give senseless advice. How can you say to Pharaoh, "I am one of the wise men, a disciple of the ancient kings"?' (19:11). We note from this verse that the wise men appear as counsellors of kings. A very important and, no doubt, lucrative job.

Wise men and the Royal Court

It was particularly to Solomon that the wise men traced their roots. Of him it is written: 'God gave Solomon wisdom and very great insight, and a breadth of understanding as measureless as the sand on the seashore. Solomon's wisdom was greater than the wisdom of all the men of the East, and greater than all the wisdom of Egypt .... He spoke three thousand proverbs .... He described plant life, from the cedar of Lebanon to the hissop that grows out of walls. He also taught about animals and birds, reptiles and fish. Men of all nations came to listen to Solomon's wisdom...' (1 Kings 4:29-34).

Note the comparison with wisdom centres in the east, i.e.

Mesopotamia, and to Egypt in the west. His court is pictured as a centre to which people from all over the world came to hear, and no doubt to share, in the jewels of wisdom. The existence of such a gathering of foreigners in Jerusalem is remarkable and marks off the wise men in a special way. We never hear of international gatherings of priests or of prophets in the city. The wise men in contrast represent human wisdom at its finest, when it is influenced by the fear of the Lord. Proverbial sayings were Solomon's special delight, but he was also knowledgeable in flora and fauna.

No other Israelite king is marked out in this way as an example of great wisdom. Rather, wise men were necessary to the royalty for their wisdom, so that the royal court was the place where wisdom was nurtured. We learn this also from sources outside the Bible. In the quote from Jeremiah above, they are noted for their 'counsel', just as the priest is noted for teaching the law, and the prophet for proclaiming the divine word.

We notice the presence and influence of men with ability in writing and giving counsel in the court of King David, 1000 BC, even before Solomon: 'Jehoshaphat ... was recorder; Shavsha was secretary ... Jonathan, David's uncle, was a counsellor, a man of insight and a scribe ... Ahitophel was the king's counsellor' (1 Chron. 18:15-17 and 27:32-33). Notice the strong emphasis on writing – recorder, secretary, scribe. 'Secretary' in the Old Testament seems to have some of the double sense it has in English (where a secretary may be no more than a computer typist, but at the same time we speak of the Secretary of State, which is a very high position), and writing led to wealth and position. They became indispensable to those who wielded power, so that then, as today, they became powerful themselves.

The Writings of the Wise Men
These are mainly to be found in the books of Proverbs, Ecclesiastes, Job and the Song of Solomon, though their shadow falls in several other parts of the Old Testament. Take, for example, Psalm 49:1-4 which sounds very much like Proverbs 1:1-6.

The Book of Proverbs

This is the basic text book of the wise men. It traces much of its forms and many of its sayings back to Solomon, but also includes Solomonic type proverbs brought together 200 years later by the wise men of the days of King Hezekiah (25:1), 'sayings of the wise' (22:17) which occupy 2 ½ chapters, and even proverbs by two non-Israelites, Agur (30:1) and King Lemuel (31:1). This last is in keeping with Wisdom's more universal character.

Proverbs is a supremely optimistic book. Wisdom, like a prophet, stands in the places where people congregate, and offers her wares to all (1:20-33). She offers the possibility of a disciplined and prudent life by giving knowledge, discretion, learning, guidance, insight, understanding and wisdom to all who will accept her (1:2-5).

In a sense the book is not overly religious. It has nothing to say about the temple or the priestly and sacrificial system. It believes that mastery of life is possible if we put a few ground rules into place. However, this fact should not be over-exaggerated, since its basic convictions is that *the fear of the LORD is the beginning of wisdom* (9:10).

Its keynote is: *Humility and the fear of the Lord bring wealth and honour and life* (22:4).

It spells out the various rewards which the good life brings:

Health	Fear the Lord and shun evil, this will bring health to your body ... (3:7, 8).
Wealth	... prosperity is the reward of the righteous (13:21)
Rank	Do you see a man skilled in his work? He will serve before kings (22:29)
Long life	Grey hair is a crown of splendour; it is attained by a righteous life (16:31)

There is indeed a great deal of wisdom in these words, but it must be stressed that these are the fruits of godliness as much as of industriousness. However, stated without qualification they can become dangerous. Proverbs were never meant to be absolute statements of truth, but general observations. Indeed, when we look at the passages in which they appear, there are often qualifying statements, to the effect that wisdom is better than wealth.

At the same time Proverbs recognises something of the perplexity of life. It calls our attention to the perverseness of the human condition. Within all human life, it seems to say, there are contradictions and inequalities: 'The poor are shunned even by their neighbours, but the rich have many friends' (14:20); 'The wealth of the rich is their fortified city, but poverty is the ruin of the poor' (10:15), and several others (18:23; 22:2). There is a sense of astonishment at these social contradictions, but there is no attempt to rectify them. We feel a lack of that fiery indignation which we find in the writings of the prophets. Social evil is contemplated, and one learns wisdom by considering it, but there is no determination to change things. Such an approach could lead to complacency, and perhaps this was why later prophets scorned the wise, as part of the power-serving elite.

Proverbs sees life as totally intelligible. A few spiritual, social and personal rules will permit one to enjoy the full fruits of life. Life can be mastered. It bubbles with assurance and optimism.

Ecclesiastes

The book of Ecclesiastes gives us the feeling of tensions among the wise men. The writer is puzzled by life, indeed he is prepared to throw down the gauntlet to his fellow thinkers. Nurtured within the schools of wisdom, he is not at all convinced that life is comprehensible: 'No-one can comprehend what goes on under the sun. Despite all his efforts to search it out, man cannot discover its meaning. Even if a wise man claims he knows, he cannot really comprehend it' (8:17). The reality of life is far more complex than the neat conclusions which the wise stressed in their short, pithy sayings.

The neat rhythms of the mastered life are often rudely and catastrophically overthrown: 'The race is not to the swift or the battle to the strong, nor does food come to the wise or wealth to the brilliant or favour to the learned; but time and chance happen to them all' (9:11). Life is riddled by strange inequities, and when one throws into the melting pot the elements of *time* and *chance*, one can never plan anything with certainty. So the following verse continues: 'Moreover, no man knows when his hour will come: As fish are caught in a cruel net, or birds are taken in a snare, so men are trapped by evil times that fall unexpectedly upon them.' Sudden disaster throws an incalculable chance element into the equation, which upsets the well-balanced rhythm. His argument reminds us of James' condemnation of those who make careful plans for 'tomorrow' when they cannot be sure what fate tomorrow will bring (James 4:13-17).

Again, the writer questions the assumption that life is based on due reward for industriousness and godliness. Hard work, so prized by Proverbs, is often fruitless: 'What does the worker gain from his toil? I have seen the burden God has laid on men' (3:9-10); or it is due to selfish motives: 'I saw that all labour and all achievement spring from man's envy of his neighbour .... Better one handful with tranquillity than two handfuls with toil and chasing after the wind' (4:4-6).

Is wickedness punished and goodness always rewarded? 'In this meaningless life of mine I have seen both of these: a righteous man perishing in his righteousness, and a wicked man living long in his wickedness .... There is something else meaningless that occurs on earth: righteous men who get what the wicked deserve, and wicked men who get what the righteous deserve' (7:15 and 8:14). Proverbs, by their very nature, tend to state general truths, but Ecclesiastes rubs our nose into the grim realities of life.

The reader might be shocked to hear me suggest a conflict of thought between two books of the Bible, but he need not be. Both points of view are valid. God does often bless the righteous and industrious in material things, yet this is not always the case, and very often the opposite is true, for reasons unknown and unknowable to us. The two positions are exemplified by a comparison of Psalms 37 and 73. The former represents the optimistic, assured view of Proverbs: 'Consider the blameless, observe the upright; there is a future for the man of peace. But all sinners will be destroyed...' (37:37). Psalm 73 is not sure that it is so simple: 'I envied the arrogant when I saw the prosperity of the wicked. They have no struggles; their bodies are healthy and strong. They are free from the burdens common to man; they are not plagued by human ills .... [by contrast] in vain have I kept my heart pure; in vain have I washed my hands in innocence. All day long I have been plagued ...' (73:3-5, 13-14).

The Book of Job is another work which challenges the easy optimism of the Wise. Proverbs is a suitable backdrop to Job, with its constant emphasis on the blessing that God pours on the righteous life: 'No harm befalls the righteous, but the wicked have their fill of trouble .... Misfortune pursues the sinner, but prosperity is the reward of the righteous' (12:21 and 13:21, and check 10:30 and 14:11 for this continual theme). Job's friends held rigidly to this point of view, and fired the full force of it at poor Job.

To begin with, Job is portrayed as a thoroughly good man, of whom God himself is justly proud. But disaster strikes his house, his home, his family, his fortune. His body is riddled with sores, and he sits on the rubbish dump outside the town, scraping his skin with pieces of broken pottery. His friends, relatives and neighbours abandon him to his fate, and even his wife refuses to sympathise with him. Children throw stones at him, and some spit in his face. By day he is burnt black by the blistering heat of the sun, and his nights are plagued by nightmares.

If ever there was a man who deserved sympathy from his friends, it was Job. But they pour him into the mould of a rigid doctrine of rewards and punishments. Since they know God blesses the righteous, it is clear that Job cannot be righteous. He is evil and thoroughly deserves his suffering, indeed God has even been gracious to him: 'Know this: God has even forgotten some of your sin' (Job 11:6).

There is not room to explore the superb intricacies of the book of Job. Suffice to say that at the end of the story God condemns the friends: 'You have not spoken of me what is right, as my servant Job has' (42:8). Their neat little explanations do not do justice to the reality of the mysteries of life, before which we can only stand in awe.

Wisdom and the Prophets of Israel

The prophets were perfectly aware of the activities of the wise men. How did they view them? Was there any contact between the two groups? Were the prophets influenced by them? Most certainly yes. We have seen at the beginning of this chapter that the prophets did not live in a closed circle, but were open to all the influences of their culture. So the poetry Amos uses is typical of the poetic forms we find in Wisdom's literature.

Among literary forms we find in Amos are some of the following:

Throughout chapter 1 and in the beginning of chapter 2 we find the phrase, *for three sins of .... even for four,* which sounds very peculiar to us, but which was a normal expression in Amos' time. The GNB modernises it, they *have sinned again and again.* It is of interest to note that this kind of expression is found outside of Amos only in the Wisdom books: 'There are three things that are never satisfied, four that never say, "Enough" .... Under three things the earth trembles, under four it cannot bear up' (Prov. 30:15, 21). 'There are six things the LORD hates, seven that are detestable to him' (Prov. 6:16). See the appendix on archaeology for examples of this form outside Israel.

A second literary form is the use of the rhetorical question: *Do horses run on the rocky crags? Does one plough there with oxen?* (Amos 6:12). The self-evident answer to these questions is 'no'. They may even seem absurd questions to us, but the rhetorical question, which expects and anticipates the 'no', is a device used by Amos to point up the absurdity of Israel's poisoning of the judicial system. In Israel the absurd becomes a reality! The style is similar to that of folk wisdom which drives home its point by striking contrasts.

Repetition is an important literary tool. We see it in the long passage of chapter 1 where each judgment on a nation is couched in exactly the same form, whilst in chapter 4 there is a catalogue of Yahweh's minor judgments on the people, again in a closely structured, repetitive form. Similarly, there are five judgment visions, the first three located together in 7:1-9, the other two heading chapters 8 and 9.

A well-known poetic form in ancient Israel was the **lament**. It is characterised by short lined rhythms, which created a sense of the awfulness of the occasion. The term is found in 5:1 and could better be translated as a dirge, or 'funeral song' (GNB). At a funeral professional mourners would sing such dirges with loud wailing and shrieks. In this case the dirge is for the death of the northern nation, *Fallen is virgin Israel, never to rise again.* Normally the prophet utters a 'word' from the Lord, so that the proclaiming of a lament would have caused a shock to his hearers. The most sustained dirge in the Old Testament is the book of Lamentations, a dirge for the destruction of Jerusalem.

There are other poetic forms and connections with the Wisdom school in the book, but these are sufficient to make our point, that Amos was conversant with the poetic forms of his people, and with the ways and writings of the Wise men.

One other thing needs to be said, and that is that there seem to be snatches of hymns in various places in the book. Just to quote one of the most striking:

> *He who forms the mountains,*
> *creates the wind,*
> *and reveals his thoughts to man,*
> *he who turns dawn to darkness,*
> *and treads the high places of the earth –*
> *the LORD God Almighty is his name* (4:13).

Did Amos say this himself? Is it an editorial addition? Many scholars feel that these snatches – 5:8-9; 8:9; 9:5-6 – are intrusions, since they do not sit easily with the text.

However, since each one is clearly designed to affirm the majesty and power of Yahweh, they may be seen as Amos' own affirmation that the God, whom he has declared will punish Israel, by bringing some great world power upon it, is perfectly able to do so. As such they needed no word of explanation to make them fit into context. Whether Amos composed them himself, or used parts of psalms he had heard in Israel, is not terribly important. They simply fitted his purpose.

The downside of the relationship between wise men and prophets is that the wise often came under the prophet's lash, alongside carnal priests and false prophets, whose efforts were directed to sustaining the actual power structures. Within a couple of decades of Amos, Isaiah affirms that, 'Those who are wise will turn out to be fools, and all their cleverness will be useless' (29:14, GNB). It is difficult to imagine that the thinking which produced the books of Proverbs, Ecclesiastes and Job could degenerate, but in this they simply followed the route of false prophets and corrupt priests.

A century after Isaiah, Jeremiah is even more antagonistic toward the wise:

> 'How can you say, "We are wise,
>   for we have the law of the LORD,"
> when actually the lying pen of the scribes
>   has handled it falsely?
> The wise will be put to shame;
>   they will be dismayed and trapped.
> Since they have rejected the word of the LORD,
>   what kind of wisdom do they have?' (8:8-9).

Here we notice that the wise men have become identified with a zeal for the law, which has reduced them to the level of simply being 'scribes'.

The reader may be surprised to find that the wise men do not appear in the Gospel stories. The simple fact is that over the centuries they had been reduced to the level of scribes whose duty it was to define and protect the scrupulous fulfilment of the Law. By the time of Jesus Jewish conservative thought identified Wisdom with the written Law.

Jesus our Wisdom

It was expected in Israel that the Messiah when he came would be endowed with the Spirit of God in extraordinary manner:

> *The Spirit of the LORD will rest on him -*
> *the Spirit of wisdom and of understanding,*
> *the Spirit of counsel and of power,*
> *the Spirit of knowledge and of the fear of the LORD*
> (Isa. 11:2).

We note here that wisdom is the first of the gifts which he received, and that 'understanding', 'counsel' and 'knowledge' are also typical of the teachings of the Wisdom schools.

The life, teachings and ministry of Jesus are seen to fulfil this Messianic function perfectly. It is the characteristic of the New Testament to take up all the lines of thought from the Old, and to affirm that they find their fullest, noblest, purest character in the Lord Jesus. So it is with wisdom. Jesus pointed to the wisdom of Solomon, through the international fame of which the Queen of Sheba came to visit him, and affirms: 'She came from the ends of the earth to listen to Solomon's wisdom, and now one greater than Solomon is here' (Luke 11:31).

Paul affirms: 'Christ [is] the power of God and the wisdom of God. For the foolishness of God is wiser than man's wisdom, and the weakness of God is stronger than man's strength' (1 Cor. 1:24-25); and to the Colossians he asserts that in Christ 'are hidden all the treasures of wisdom and knowledge' (2:3). The latter example is interesting because the context is the danger to the new

Christians of high-sounding rhetoric from false teachers who appealed to their own special knowledge and wisdom.

We see the same antagonism toward the arrogance of so-called wise people of this world, which we have already seen in the prophets and in Paul, in the telling words of Jesus: 'I praise you, Father, Lord of heaven and earth, because you have hidden these things from the wise and learned, and revealed them to little children' (Matt. 11:25). True wisdom is not found in the merely secular learning of this world. This tends to breed arrogance and rejection of the Christ. Rather it is available only to those who have come to Jesus with the meekness of children, admitting they don't know, and seeking wisdom from God through his Son, Jesus the Messiah.

'I don't understand, don't understand!' lies at the heart of the Teacher's message in Ecclesiastes. Had he lived at a later time, he would surely have found the answer to his longing in the Lord Jesus Christ.

6

Amos and the Powerful

An Introduction to the
Sociology of the Old Testament

All societies require some structure in order to function adequately. Amos shows himself fully aware of the hierarchies of the nation to which he preached, and he gives us brief, but clear glimpses of the power structures, the pecking orders, which prevailed in ancient Israel, and of the way in which powerful people exploited their positions for personal gain.

The King. A fleeting remark points us to the pinnacle of power in the land, the king. Amos speaks of a vision in which he saw a swarm of locusts invading the land *after the king's share had been harvested* (7:1). The king had the royal prerogative to claim the firstfruit of the harvest, as a form of taxation. This is a very serious matter.

In biblical law the firstfruits of the land were to be brought to the Lord in the temple, as a recognition of his sovereignty (Deut. 26:1-10). Effectively the king usurped the place of the Lord, and practically speaking kingship demanded strong centralization of power, with the necessary infrastructure to sustain this, which in turn required a heavy tax burden on the common people. Amos' remark assumes this had become the norm.

Later in the same chapter Amaziah, the priest of Bethel, reported Amos' preaching at that shrine, and requests his expulsion (7:10-11). The king was the one power who could get rid of this nuisance preacher, and, though the account does not spell this out, the fact that Amos' prophecy is limited to one year would suggest that the king had him escorted back to his native Judah, perhaps with some lack of dignity.

Amos has little to say about the king, but within a decade Hosea, a native of the north, did not mix his words in denouncing kingship. He accuses the king and the whole royal family of being leaders in the general debauchery that marked the upper crust of society: 'On the day of the festival of our king the princes become inflamed with wine and he joins hands with the mockers' (Hosea 7:5). In fact Hosea is persuaded that the whole nature of kingship in Israel was a fatal mistake, for he jeers at the inability of the king to deliver his people from the coming threat of destruction: 'You are destroyed, O Israel .... Where is your king, that he may save you?.... of whom you said, "Give me a king and princes"? So in my anger I gave you a king, and in my wrath I took him away' (13:9-11). He is convinced that terminal destruction is the only end result for the nation's kingship: 'Samaria and its king will float away like a twig on the surface of the waters' (10:7).

The Priests. Amos' confrontation with Amaziah is a classic example of the difficulties which the true prophets had with the priesthood. They were often infuriated at the state of things within the temple, even the Lord's temple in Jerusalem. Isaiah begins his ministry with a total rejection of what he sees happening in the Jerusalem temple (Isa. 1:10-15). It is not that he is against the temple. He himself received a vision of God in the temple and it was there that the Lord called him to service (Isa. 6:1-7).

But when Isaiah saw that the apparently pious activities – prayer, singing, worship – were divorced from goodness of life, he was furious. His God says to the people through him: 'When you spread your hands out in prayer, I will hide my eyes from you; even if you offer many prayers, I will not listen. Your hands are full of blood' (Isa. 1:15). On another occasion he accuses them: 'On the day of your fasting .... you exploit all your workers. Your fasting ends in quarrelling and strife, and in striking each other with wicked fists' (Isa. 58:3-4).

Since the priests were the powerful people in religion they are held chiefly responsible for the break up of the moral life of the people. Hosea, writing very shortly after Amos, lays the chief blame for this at the feet of the priests: 'The more the priests increased, the more they sinned against me; they exchange their Glory for something disgraceful. They feed on the sins of my people and relish their wickedness' (Hosea 4:7). Instead of being the conscience of the nation, they absorbed the evil around them, and these institutional priests lived lives very little different from the most corrupt.

It is always a grave danger when the church panders to the powers that be. Instead of fulfilling its prophetic role it lends its sanction to these same exploiters. The powerful themselves often feel the need of acceptance and justification from religion, but the price to the godly is disastrous. Short term gains become disastrous losses in the long term, when the church is expected to lend its full support to the powers.

The Merchants. In chapter 8 Amos turns on the wealthy merchants, who are always out to make a quick buck at the expense of the poor: *Hear this, you who trample the needy and do away with the poor of the land, saying, 'When will the New Moon be over that we may sell grain, and the Sabbath be ended that we may market wheat?'* and as if impatience with religious activities which get in the way of commercial gain (how modern!) were not enough, he accuses them of *Skimping the measure, boosting the price and cheating with dishonest scales, buying the poor with silver and the needy for a pair of sandals, selling even the sweepings with the wheat* (8:4-6).

The Judges. The law court is the ultimate refuge of those who feel defrauded, but as so often happens in human history, the judges also are very human and not infrequently open to the highest bidder. Amos devotes most of chapter 5 to a confrontation with the powerful precisely over this fact. He accuses the leaders of *turning justice into bitterness and casting righteousness to the ground* (verse 7). We shall see later that these two words, 'justice' and 'righteousness', are the key elements in a solution of the problems of humans living together in society.

It seems to be to the poor man's lawyer, or perhaps to the ordinary citizen who was angered by what was going on, that Amos refers when he says: *You hate the one who reproves in court and despise him who tells the truth* (verse 10). Anyone who came to the help of the poor being milched by the system, was likely to find himself in the bad books of the powerful, who had the legal system in their pockets, literally. Furiously Amos cries – and it seems that only the prophets had the courage to do this – *You oppress the righteous and take bribes and you deprive the poor of justice in the courts* (verse 12), with the result that even those who were scandalised by these acts, held their peace for fear of reprisals (verse 13).

No doubt the judges' pockets were well lined by those who bribed them. It is interesting and important to notice that in Psalm 82 the judges are said to be like 'gods'. In a unique sense the judge holds the balance of truth and rightness in a society, which is in itself a divine faculty. When he fails, the whole system fails. So the psalmist rounds on false judges: 'How long will you defend the unjust, and show partiality to the wicked? Defend the cause of the weak and fatherless; maintain the rights of the poor and oppressed. Rescue the weak and needy; deliver them from the hand of the wicked' (82:2-4). The fact that these words were sung in the temple shows how vitally they represented the faith of Israel at its finest. Tragically they were being denied by the very people who sang the words!

Landowners. This is a class of people who are not singled out by Amos, though they will be recognizable in other ways. It is Micah, a man from a small country town, who blasts these exploiters: 'Woe to those who plan iniquity, to those who plot evil on their beds! At morning light they carry it out because it is in their power to do it. They covet fields and seize them, and houses, and take them. They defraud a man of his home, a fellow-man of his inheritance .... You drive the women of my people from their pleasant homes. You take away my blessing from their children for ever' (Micah 2:1-2, 9). Protective property laws in favour of the poor and the weak were written into the nation's constitution, but these rapacious landowners had no regard for them.

Prophets. Again, Amos has little to say about these, though he recognised that the prophets were in the unfortunate position of having pressure put on them to accommodate their message to present trends: *You ... commanded the prophets not to prophesy* (2:12). We shall look more closely at the prophets in our last chapter, but here it is important to notice that as pressure was brought on them to support the powerful leaders, so their lives became conformed to the level of these evil men.

Micah singles out these 'false' prophets as worthy of divine anger: 'This is what the LORD says: "As for the prophets who lead my people astray, if one feeds them, they proclaim 'peace'; if he does not, they prepare to wage war against him" ' (Micah 3:5). It was an embarrassment for the corrupted prophet to meet up with true prophets. It spoke so deeply to their consciences that they lashed out against them. Jeremiah found these people the worst to handle. The classic passage on this theme is found in Jeremiah 23:9-40.

The Leaders of the Nation. Amos 6 begins with a graphic picture of the style of life to which the people occupying positions of power had become accustomed in Israel. He describes them as the *notable men of the foremost nation, to whom the people of Israel come* (6:1). These were the natural leaders of the country, from whom the people expected leadership, and to whom they looked for an example. They were clearly the nobility, the priests, merchants, judges, landowners, and false prophets whom we have seen thus far. For them leadership meant the possibility of enrichment, of a care-free lifestyle. Amos blasts their luxury:

> *You lie on beds inlaid with ivory*
> *   and lounge on your couches.*
> *You dine on choice lambs*
> *   and fattened calves.*
> *You strum away on your harps like David*
> *   and improvise on musical instruments.*
> *You drink wine by the bowlful*
> *   and use the finest lotions* (6:4-6).

Here indeed were a people who had it made, who enjoyed the sweet life. Israel and Judah were at the height of material prosperity during this period. Their lands stretched from the Gulf of Eilat to regions north of Damascus, approaching the River Euphrates. All the small lands around them brought tribute, effectively paid taxes to them, and these could have been days of material well-being for all the people. But it was not so.

We have seen how Amos in chapters 1 and 2 hits out at the nations around Israel for the way in which they have crushed other peoples. But in the case of Israel the accusation is not that they have crushed other peoples, but that they have crushed their own people. In fact the luxury lifestyle of the rich was made possible by riding roughshod over the rights of the poor, of their fellow countrymen. Some few years later Isaiah could put it more bluntly: 'The plunder from the poor is in your houses ...' (Isa. 3:14). Their high lifestyle was sustained by taxes and fines imposed on the poor.

The key passage in this respect is the conclusion of the string of accusations in 2:6-7, where Amos affirms: *They sell the righteous for silver, and the needy for a pair of sandals.* This points to debt slavery. Where a person could not pay their debts they could pay them off by working for the creditor. This might not be a bad system, but could easily be exploited to obtain cheap labour. So the accusation here is that they sell honest citizens for the most trivial debts. They have become avaricious in building up their own material comforts, and have not hesitated to exploit and crush the poor in order to do so.

They trample on the heads of the poor, continues Amos, *as upon the dust of the ground and deny justice to the oppressed.* Nothing will stop them in their frenetic haste to accumulate power, prestige and wealth. Rapacious creditors joined with corrupt judges to exploit the debts of honest people.

A generation later, Micah could accuse even the wealthy of Jerusalem of the same evil. As we have seen, people who hold the reins of power do not hesitate to use it to further their own interests (Micah 2:1-2).

The Women. It was the men who held the reins of power in ancient Israel, but behind them stood wives, with their incessant demands for a more comfortable lifestyle. Amos turns against these women in 4:1, with a very unflattering description: *Hear this word, you cows of Bashan on Mount Samaria, you women who oppress the poor and crush the needy and say to your husbands, 'Bring us some drinks!'* Incessant nagging of the powerful men by their materialistic wives, led them to exploitation which possibly they might otherwise have been reluctant to pursue.

Isaiah has a blistering attack on these same oppressors, humorous if it wasn't so sad for the poor people: 'The women of Zion are haughty, walking along with outstretched necks, flirting with their eyes, tripping along with mincing steps, with ornaments jingling on their ankles' (Isa. 3:16).

Violence and **Oppression.** Amos uses graphic language to describe the way in which the weak are being treated. Three times he accuses the powerful of 'trampling' on the poor

The words 'oppress', 'oppression', etc., in our English Bibles are translations of more than 20 words in Hebrew, and one of these alone is variously translated into English in more than 50 ways. In its verb form we find: afflict, oppress, humble, subdue, mistreat, rape, violate; and in its noun form: poor, helpless, needy, humble, meek, wretched. The richness of vocabulary stresses the importance of these words in the experience of the people. This nation had once experienced horrific oppression at the hands of foreigners, the Egyptians, now they were suffering oppression at the hands of their own countrymen.

Listen to the Teacher in Ecclesiastes 4:1: 'Again I looked and saw all the oppression that was taking place under the sun: I saw the tears of the oppressed – and they have no comforter; power was on the side of their oppressors – and they have no comforter.' Note the pathos of these words. They express something of both distress in the mind of the beholder, and of perplexity. Far from the fiery indignation of the prophets, there is even a note of despair, as the writer goes on to say that 'the dead who had already died are happier than the living'.

We may sum up this section by saying that Amos and his fellow prophets saw the cruel way in which their society had become divided between the 'haves' and the 'have-nots', and that the former, so far from being satisfied with their privileged lot, used their positions of power to feather their own nests. We will ask Micah, the hill-billy preacher from the little-known village of Moresheth, to sum it up in his very graphic fashion: 'Listen, you leaders of Jacob, you rulers of the house of Israel ... you who hate good and love evil; who tear the skin from my people and the flesh from their bones; who eat my people's flesh, strip off their skin and break their bones in pieces; who chop them up like meat for the pan, like flesh for the pot' (Micah 3:1-3).

It was not always so

Some 500 years before Amos' days the Israelites had emerged on the world stage as a gang of runaway slaves, who overthrew the inhabitants of Canaan and established themselves as a nation. They had no doubt that this land was given to them graciously by Yahweh their God.

Here in this land they began a remarkable social experiment. Theodore Robinson, a Bible scholar, affirmed in 1927: 'Except in her conception of religion Israel had no greater gift to offer to the world than this, a truly democratic theory of the relation between the government and the governed.'[1] Democracy? Surely that's a thoroughly modern concept. Well, let's see.

The first social act Israel performed in conquered Canaan was a division of the land among their own tribes, clans and families. The book of Joshua spends nine chapters, ten pages in my Bible, which must surely be counted among the most 'boring' in the whole book. Joshua 13-21 give details of the exact division of the land among the clans. Each clan and family gets a portion of land based on the principle of equality, with its border carefully spelt out. The modern reader may be pardoned for finding these details of unknown valleys and hills uninspiring, but they demonstrate that Israel had the conviction that originally the land had been distributed equitably among its people.

This fact has been disputed by some. Is this merely a utopian vision of a wonderful past? One can at least say for certain that Israel conserved a knowledge of its past, that in the beginning everything had been done on the basis of equality. Remember that they had been slaves, sweat labour for massive Egyptian building projects. Proudly they now asserted their independence, and their determination to live as equals, and never to exploit each other.

This determination was enshrined in laws, which the Israelites had received at Mt. Sinai en route to the promised land. Their constitution, if we may call it that, was grounded on the 10 Commandments, recorded in Exodus 20. They are to be found in many ancient English churches, which show the profound impact that these had on Western law. Alongside laws against blasphemy, adultery, theft and murder, were those which required respect for one's family relationships, and the last which ran, 'You shall not covet your neighbour's house. You shall not covet your

---

[1]T. H. Robinson, *Palestine in General History* (Schweich Lectures, 1929), p.41.

neighbour's wife, or his manservant or maidservant, his ox or donkey, or anything that belongs to your neighbour.' The reader will appreciate how far this was from the rapacious rulers of Amos' and Micah's days.

These general laws were then applied in a series of specific laws to be followed by the people in the particular conditions in which they would find themselves once they were in the land. There is not space or necessity to spell these out in detail, but one will give the general ethos: 'Do not take advantage of a widow or an orphan. If you do and they cry out to me, I will certainly hear their cry. My anger will be aroused, and I will kill you with the sword; your wives will become widows and your children fatherless' (Exod. 22:22-24).

Many of these laws will sound to the modern reader archaic, simplistic, and impossible of application in modern society, and of course one would never suggest such a possibility. However, the important thing to notice is that behind the specific laws we can detect the mind of God, his likes and dislikes, his concerns, indeed his very nature. It is true that their laws are not our laws, as Paul so firmly insisted in the New Testament, but behind them stands the mind of the same God whom we worship. He did not cook up these laws arbitrarily for the Israelites. God can do nothing arbitrary or capricious. He is for ever unchangeably the same.

Perhaps the most astonishing set of laws within the system given to Israel was that relating to land. Remember the land had been distributed on the basis of equality among all the families. However, people who are potentially equal in the sight of God and of society, are not so in reality. The book of Proverbs pours scorn on the idle: 'I went past the field of the sluggard ... thorns had come up everywhere, the ground was covered with weeds, and the stone wall was in ruins. I applied my heart to what I observed and learned a lesson from what I saw: a little sleep, a little slumber, a little folding of the hands to rest – and poverty will come on you like a bandit and scarcity like an armed man' (Prov. 24:30-34). The sluggard is a morally irresponsible person, whose poverty is the consequence of his own condition.

There were many causes of poverty: laziness, drunkenness, crime, poor harvests, injustice and exploitation, or sheer bad luck. There were always those who just couldn't make it, and who found themselves and their families in such difficult financial conditions that they were forced to sell their one important family asset – land – and there would always be buyers.

Land - Wot! No Freehold?

In modern Western society the concept of freehold property rights is virtually a sacred concept. Astonishingly, in Israel it was looked at differently. Three laws were introduced designed to protect family land. The law recognised that poverty would force people to sell land, but these rules were introduced to restrict abuse.

Firstly, if family property was put up for sale, it was the moral obligation of a near relative to buy the land, so as to keep it within the context of the wider family relationships, called the clan. This was not, however, always possible, since the case could be given where the near relative either did not want to buy it, or simply did not have the economic capacity to do so.

The second law stipulated that if the original owner's financial condition subsequently improved and he found himself in the position of being able to buy back the property, the new owner is obliged to return it to him. Now here is the sting in this tail. So far from receiving more for the resale, as we would expect today, whether through higher property values or through inflation, he was to receive less. Since he had had the use of the land over x number of years, these years were discounted from the price and he received a lesser value.

But maybe neither of these things would happen and the new owner, probably of another clan or tribe, or even a resident foreigner, would hold the land for decades. So a third law came into operation. Every 50th year all land was to revert back to its original owner. This was not 50 years after the sale, but a specific year when it was to happen all over the country, called the Year of Jubilee, details of which will be found in Leviticus 25. At first glance this might all seem like a premium on laziness! But it must be remembered that in all probability the original owner was dead, or at least in advanced age, so that the beneficiaries were the family members, not the individual.

Thus we might say in modern terminology that there was no freehold sale of land. All land and property could only be sold on a leasehold basis and its value would depend on the number of years to the next Jubilee Year. The net result of these laws was, on the one side, to restrict the possibility of families being snared in the poverty trap, and on the other hand, of restricting vast accumulation of land in the hands of the wealthy. An integral part of the scheme was the existence of the clan, whose duty it was to protect the land interests of their extended-family members.

It will be asked whether these laws were ever enforced. Our danger here is of thinking in terms of the nation-state of modern times. Israel existed in the early days as numerous small towns and villages, each of which enjoyed a fairly comprehensive autonomy. So the enforcement will have been principally at a local level. The little book of Ruth is a gem which shows that, whilst in many places evil had destroyed the system, there were pockets around the country where the old system of freedom and equality still held sway.

It is easy to assume that in these laws Israel was merely imitating the systems which held in ancient times, but there is evidence to the contrary. The Canaanite pre-Israelite towns, of which we know a great deal through archaeological evidence, had been characterised by a strong centralist tendency. Rulers in the big towns dominated over as wide an area as possible. Strong taxation systems on rural farmers were the norm. The city authorities in their turn had to pay heavy tribute to the over-ruling empire power, usually Egypt. Early Israel introduced a de-centralised, remarkably democratic, way of life.

We want a King! – a pivotal point in Israel's history

In one of the most important chapters in the Old Testament, 1 Samuel 8, the people demanded that Samuel install a monarchy to lead the nation: *'appoint a king to lead us, such as all the other nations have'* (verse 5). The last phrase is notable. The people here recognised that their system was fundamentally different from all other nations. It was, we might say, a simple form of democracy, where local people made the decisions which vitally affected their lives and happiness.

Now the people were turning from this and demanding the same kind of systems which prevailed in all other peoples. Reluctantly Samuel bowed to their wishes, but solemnly declared to them the consequences of their demand:

> This is what the king who will reign over you will do: he will take your sons and make them serve with his chariots and horses, and they will run in front of his chariots. Some he will assign to be commanders of thousands and commanders of fifties, and others to plough his ground and reap his harvest, and still others to make weapons of war and equipment for his chariots. He will take your daughters to be perfumers, and cooks, and bakers. He will take the best of your fields and vineyards and olive groves, and give them to his attendants. Your menservants and maidservants and the best of your cattle and donkeys he will take for his own use. He will take a tenth of your flock, and you yourselves will become his slaves (1 Sam. 8:11-17).

I have quoted the passage in full because it is very important. If we could sum up the consequences of kingship which Samuel is warning them of, in one word it would be *exploitation*. He was saying that precisely that order of things which Amos paints for us 300 years later, would be brought into operation through the people's demands for kingship. It is a sombre thought that apparent short-term gains – the defence of the country against Philistine oppression – would have dire consequences in the long run.

The king begins by undermining family life, separating sons and daughters from their natural home contexts, reducing them to a condition of total dependence on the state. He would be characterised by land grabbing, and the people would be subjected to heavy taxes to support the monarchy, its nobility, and its bureaucratic structures. Let's see what happened.

Strangely the process begins with the hero David, and that on two fronts, land and military leaders. David's family land was located in the little town of Bethlehem. Yet we find him needing a large number of overseers to care for his extensive properties (1 Chron. 27:25-31). The simple shepherd boy looking after family sheep has become a powerful landowner, which one presumes must have been expropriated from other people in some way or other.

His predecessor, King Saul, had started a small army, and archaeological remains at his capital, Gibeah, show that his palace was basically an army barracks. David, even before he became king, had gathered 600 armed men, most of whom had fallen foul of the law. On taking the kingship in a nasty power struggle, his bodyguard was largely composed of Gittites, Philistines from Gath, to which town he had earlier related as a dependent freebooter, heading an armed gang. Most surprising, by the time his army, with its many feats of conquest, had reached its maximum power the two generals who headed it, Joab and Abishai, were nephews of David, sons of his sister, Zeruiah. Asahel, another nephew, appears to have been advancing well, but was killed by Saul's former army general and relative, Abner, later himself murdered by Joab. Clearly David's intention was to keep power within his own clan.

But the real transformation, from a simple form of democracy, in which local people exercised a great deal of autonomy, was reached by Solomon. Here it is necessary to note that the Bible often tells us incidents with a minimum or no commentary, and expects us to make moral judgments, informed by what we already know of God's ways.

Thus in 2 Chronicles 2:17 Solomon made a census of all the 'aliens' resident in Israel, and set them to hard labour on his expensive building projects, putting foremen over them, 'to keep the people working'. Now the simplest Bible reader is expected to remember that the people of Israel had been aliens in Egypt, that they had been put to hard labour on the Pharaoh's building projects, and that foremen had been placed over them to ensure that they worked very hard. However, the historian does not himself make the comparison. He expects us to use the knowledge we already have of God's ways. The Bible makes clear that the heart of the God of Israel was moved to compassion on those thus brutally treated. So here with the brutality of Solomon in his treatment of aliens.

It seems that the whole story of Solomon is told in a satirical manner, with the reader expected to make his own judgment on the basis of the evidence. He is the wisest of men, but what wisdom is this that ends up destroying his own nation? Here was a man who could dedicate a temple to the Lord, but a double-minded man, flirting with pagan gods. Here was a man who accumulated great wealth, but what kind of economist was he who ended up bankrupting his people?

The exploitation which began with aliens soon moved to include his own compatriots: 'Solomon conscripted labourers from all Israel .... Adoniram was in charge of the forced labour' (1 Kings 5:13-18). This labour was in the form of corvée, a system whereby every Israelite male was obliged to give one month in every three as unpaid labour to the state. Basically the work consisted of quarrying and moving large blocks of stone for Solomon's big building projects, back-breaking work like that of their forefathers in Egyptian slavery.

The law of Israel had anticipated a time when Israel would demand a king, and Moses left instructions as to how the king was to rule. He was expected to be an example of a pious and godly Israelite, copying his own book of the law, and keeping a copy with him every day, in which to meditate, reflect and pray.

On the negative side he was warned of those things which are a king's temptation – he was not to accumulate wealth, nor wives, nor trade in any way with the Egyptians, from whom the Israelites had fled. You will see from this that Solomon broke every rule in the book (see Deuteronomy 17:14-20).

As a direct result of Solomon's folly the country was split into two, Israel in the north, Judah in the south, a breach which was never to be healed. The story of two lines of kingship which followed over the next 300 years, with a few bright exceptions, is dismal.

However, the old system of early Israel was not destroyed overnight. Rather there was an ongoing tension between the old democracy, and the new centralised power. The prophets were not the only ones who saw the abuses caused by centralised power. Listen to the Preacher, author of Ecclesiastes: 'If you see the poor oppressed in a district, and justice and rights denied, do not be surprised at such things; for one official is eyed by a higher one, and over them both are others higher still. The increase of the land is taken by all; the king himself profits from the fields' (4:8-9). Here truly is a hierarchy of power, with each level envious of the wealth and power of the one above it.

The way back to God

Though evil had come in like a flood, and our friend Amos despaired of his people, yet he knew there was a solution to the problem. His basic accusation is that those in power were guilty of *denying* justice *to the oppressed* (2:7). At 6:12 he expresses the incredible scandal of Israel: *Do horses run on the rocky crags? Does one plough there with oxen? But you have turned* justice *into poison and the fruit of* righteousness *into bitterness*. His two questions here expect the answer: Of course not, and his *But you have...* implies that what is incredible in the natural realm is precisely what Israel has done in the social and moral realm. In the key passage in chapter 5 he accuses them: *You turn* justice *into bitterness and cast* righteousness *to the ground* (5:7). This they do by *depriving the poor of justice in the courts* (5:12).

His answer to their condition is on the one side to reject all their false hopes and pretended religion. Their false hopes lay in the fact that they considered themselves to be the privileged people of God, free from all condemnation. This is graphically portrayed by the prophet Micah: 'Her leaders judge for a bribe, her priests teach for a price, and her prophets tell fortunes for money. Yet they lean upon the LORD and say, "Is not the LORD among us? No disaster will come upon us" ' (3:11). Amos rejected the popular expectation of the Day of the Lord, as a day in which Israel's enemies would be destroyed, and Israel gloriously saved. He says that all sinners, pagans or Israelites, would be punished on that day (5:18-20).

Amos turns furiously on their religion. These powerful people trooped to the temple on the Sabbath to sing the Lord's praises. Amos rejects all this. He hears the Lord say: *I hate, I despise your religious feasts; I cannot stand your assemblies ... Away with the noise of your songs! I will not listen to the music of your harps* (5:21-23), and then he utters the key to his whole message:

**Let justice roll on like a river,
righteousness like a never-failing stream.**

There seem to me to be two graphic figures here. There is an intended contrast between the sporadic torrents of water which rush down the mountainside in times of rain, but which for the most part are empty of any water at all, and the constant stream which emanates from an unfailing spring. What Amos demands is that they shall bring in justice and righteousness in full flood, and keep it going constantly.

Yahweh, the God of Israel despises religion, even though he is its object, when it is divorced from goodness of life, from kindness to one's fellows, from the reign of justice. It is only the re-establishment of justice in the land which will serve as an insurance policy against the wrath of God.

Ruanda and the 'Blessing'

30 years ago, when I was a young man, Ruanda was the place to go to for a blessing. Wonderful stories circulated among evangelical churches about the things God was doing in that country. Sadly, in 1994 Ruanda erupted in one of the most terrible events of the 20th century. The most evangelised country in Africa exploded in ethnic violence. I do not pretend to explain how this came about, but the certainty is that something was lacking in the Christian message.

These events have caused much heart-searching in missionary circles. 'Ruanda', wrote the prestigious *Evangelical Missions Quarterly*, 'has shaken the world missions community to its roots ... What kind of gospel are we preaching?' The fact is that if our gospel does not produce changed lives which long to see justice and righteousness enthroned among men, then some form of disaster will always follow in its wake. We may profess to have the latest 'blessing' on offer, but Christ will have nothing less than changed daily lives.

Justice and Righteousness

You will have noticed that these two words are found together frequently. In fact, they are so important that they appear more than 1,000 times in the Old Testament. This frequency says something to us about God's priorities. Micah insisted that what God requires of man is, *'To do justice, to love mercy, and to walk humbly with your God'* (6:8). Centuries later Jesus rejected the piety of the Pharisees in their scrupulous observance of the minute details of the tithing laws, and accused them of passing over the weighty matters of the Law: justice, mercy and faithfulness (Matt. 23:23), which sounds like a quotation from Micah. Jesus was saying that God has priorities and these are what they are. On another occasion he said: 'In everything, do to others as you would have them do to you, for this sums up the Law and the Prophets' (Matt. 7:12). 'The Law and the Prophets' here is simply a way of saying 'the Old Testament'. So he means that the distilled essence of the Old Testament message is the question of how we should relate to each other.

Not only do these two words, justice and righteousness, appear more than 1,000 times in the Old Testament, they frequently appear together. Look at the following examples:

'The LORD reigns ... *righteousness* and *justice* are the foundation of his throne' (Psalm 97:1-2). This is food for thought. The king of the universe bases all his actions and relationships on these principles. They are the law of the universe. In which case anything else is the law of the jungle!

'I am the LORD, who exercises kindness, *justice* and *righteousness* on earth, for in these I delight' (Jer. 9:24). These qualities are those which God exercises himself, and which he delights to see happening.

'I will make *justice* the measuring line and *righteousness* the plumb line' (Isa. 28:17). God measures all human activity on the basis of these qualities.

We see from these examples, and they can be found over and over again, that justice and righteousness are the basis of all God's activities and all his concerns with mankind. How much more with his chosen people, Israel.

In a striking passage we learn that Isaiah took his guitar, or whatever equivalent he had, and went to a wine festival. He played to the people the song of a vineyard, on which the owner had spent much time and effort, but when he came to look for sweet grapes, he could find only wild, sour grapes. So he decided to destroy the vineyard. Having obtained a hearing Isaiah turned on his listeners and told them that they were the Lord's vineyard, his delightful garden, 'and he looked for *justice*, but saw bloodshed; for *righteousness*, but heard cries of distress' (Isa. 5:7). God came looking for justice and righteousness, and he was angry because he could not find it. Notice that he did not look for more prayer, attendance at worship, or Bible study, but more justice and righteousness. These words record the divine disappointment with Israel and are a resumé of divine intent and human failure, a tangible version of the creation story.

There then follows in Isaiah 5:8-22 a catalogue of the 'sour grapes' which the Lord found in Israel, with the pivotal statement in verse 16: 'But the LORD Almighty will be exalted by *justice*, and the holy God will show himself holy by *righteousness*.'

So, justice and righteousness stand at the core of divine Being. They are the evidence of his presence, his requirements for human society. In failing to produce them, Israel had wrongly represented him before the nations. The disappointment of God then turns to anger (Isa. 5: 24-25).

But what are Justice and Righteousness?

First, a word of warning. By New Testament times 'righteousness' had come to be equated with showy religious acts, basically, giving to charity, prayer, and fasting. These were done openly, in order to impress people with one's piety. Of these Jesus said: 'Be careful not to do your "acts of righteousness" before men, to be seen by them' (Matt. 6:1).

The Old Testament prophets meant something very different by these terms. N. Snaith defined 'righteousness' as the 'norm in the affairs of the world to which men and things should conform, and by which they can be measured'.[2] The Hebrew word is translated 'honest' in Leviticus 19:36 which is an excellent example: 'Use honest scales, honest weights, and honest measures' (GNB). Other translations here translate it as 'true', 'accurate'. In the moral and social sphere it signifies things as they ought to be.

In contrast the word 'justice' is the process of law, verdict, judgment. In the plural form it means 'laws, statutes'. So in giving the detailed requirements of the law in Exodus 21-23, the passage

[2]N. Snaith, *The Distinctive Ideas of the Old Testament* (Epworth Press, 1944), p.73.

begins: 'These are the laws...' (21:1). The English obscures the fact that the word means 'judicial requirements'. Thus 'justice' refers to specific acts marking out man's dealings with his fellow men.

But the two words are closely wedded to each other. Justice must be informed by righteousness, but righteousness must be expressed through just acts. In God's eyes, you cannot be a righteous person if you do unjust acts. Piety cannot be divorced from the context of social responsibility, the way we relate to each other, whether in Christian or in human society. I would define the two words together as meaning 'finely-tuned justice'.

God is concerned primarily about how people relate in society, both within his chosen community, the church, and within society in general. If people do not know how to relate to each other in family, church, community and nation, then that is very bad news. Yet at all these levels modern society seems to tear itself apart, and the church is not immune from it.

The yearning for this two-in-one quality pervades every aspect of Old Testament teaching. As we have seen it is the passion of the prophets, with its inclination in particular support of the weak and poor of society, who are most likely to be exploited – widows, orphans, slaves, aliens. In this the prophets were no more than echoing the themes spelt out in Israel's ancient laws.

It is also found in Israel's song-book, the Psalms, where Psalm 72 is a description of the requirements of kingship: 'Endow the king with your *justice*, O God, the royal son with your *righteousness*. He will judge your people in *righteousness*, your afflicted ones with *justice*' (verses 1-2); and this justice is to incline in favour of the poor and weak: 'He will defend the afflicted among the people and save the children of the needy; he will crush the oppressor .... He will deliver the needy who cry out, the afflicted who have no-one to help. He will take pity on the weak and the needy, and save the needy from death. He will rescue them from oppression and violence' (verses 4, 12-14).

The wise men of the book of Proverbs also looked to justice

and righteousness. Thus 8:20 depicts Wisdom explaining her true route: 'I walk in the ways of *righteousness*, along the paths of *justice*.' In general, since proverbial sayings by their very character deal with general principles rather than particular cases, the word *righteousness* is preferred in the book, and *justice* is scarce. Consider: 'You will walk in the ways of good men and keep to the paths of the righteous' (2:20); 'He who sows righteousness reaps a sure reward' (11:18); 'The LORD ... loves those who pursue righteousness' (15:9).

Fascinatingly, Proverbs even brings in a non-Israelite king, Lemuel, as an ideal for the exercise of power and justice in favour of the beleaguered poor: 'Speak up for those who cannot speak for themselves, for the rights of all who are destitute. Speak up and judge fairly; defend the rights of the poor and needy' (31:1-9), though in all fairness it must be pointed out that it was his mother who taught him these principles!

When the prophets dreamt of that coming day when Messiah would come and establish his kingdom, it was essentially one where justice and righteousness would be finally enthroned on earth:

Isaiah cries: 'He will reign on David's throne and over his kingdom, establishing and upholding it with *justice* and *righteousness* from that time on and for ever'; '... with *righteousness* he will judge the needy, with *justice* he will give decisions for the poor of the earth'; 'He will bring *justice* to the nations ... in faithfulness he will bring forth *justice*; he will not falter or be discouraged till he establishes *justice* on earth' (Isa. 9:7; 11:4; 42:1-4).

A century after Isaiah, Jeremiah dreams of the day of Messiah's coming, and exclaims: 'In those days and at that time I will make a righteous Branch sprout from David's line: he will do what is just and right in the land .... This is the name by which he will be called: The LORD Our Righteousness (Jer. 33:15-16).

There can be no Peace without justice and righteousness
Other words cluster around justice and righteousness. Biblical
scholar Chris Wright calls these 'harmonics'. Psalm 89:14 affirms:
'Righteousness and justice are the foundation of your throne; *love*
and *faithfulness* go before you.' The word for 'love' has been
variously translated 'mercy', loving kindness', 'steadfast love'.
It is associated with the idea of a covenant, like a marriage, in
which both sides agree to be faithful to each other. Loyal love is
what the Lord covenants to give to Israel, this is also the quality
which he expects from them. Faithfulness is a kindred idea. It is
often found in conjunction with love and truth (Psalm 89:1,2).

The end purpose of all human society from a biblical
perspective is *peace – shalom*. Shalom is humankind in perfect
harmony with itself and with its conditions. Obviously, it is only
attainable in a measure. The problem is that it is often virtually
non-existent, which is the great pain of the prophets. There are, of
course, false offers, false solutions, which offer peace, but in fact
do not achieve it. The false prophets 'dress the wound of my people
as though it were not serious. "Peace, peace," they say, when there
is no peace' (Jer. 6:14 and 8:11).

The psalmist affirms that God 'promises peace to his people
.... Surely his salvation is near those who fear him .... Love and
faithfulness meet together; righteousness and peace kiss each
other' (Psalm 85:8-10). Amos' cry that righteousness and justice
must flow like a river bursting its banks, is born out of the certainty
that peace is only possible in a society where man's search for
happiness and fulfilment is linked to truth, faithfulness, love,
righteousness and justice.

Jesus and Amos

In Jesus God stands 'sociologically' on the side of the weak, the
poor, the handicapped, the oppressed. He identified in every aspect
of his life with the poor, so that the common people heard him
gladly, whilst the powerful put him to death. These words of the

renowned Dutch Christian, Abraham Kuyper, are a suitable climax to this chapter:

> When rich and poor stand opposed to each other, Jesus never takes his place with the wealthier, but always stands with the poorer. He is born in a stable; and while foxes have holes and birds have nests, the Son of Man has nowhere to lay his head .... Both the Christ, and also as much the apostles after him as the prophets before him, invariably took sides against those who were powerful and living in luxury, and for the suffering and oppressed. [3]

---

[3]Abraham Kuyper, *Christianity and the Class Struggle* (Grand Rapids, 1950), pp. 27-28, 50.

7

Amos the Visionary

An Anticipation of Jesus?

The first verse of chapter 1 is editorial. Whether it was written by an immediate disciple/admirer or a later editor is not important. It demonstrates that, in spite of his own statements in chapter 7, he was quickly classified among the group of men known in ancient Israel as 'prophets'. Not that this term is used in the verse, but the concepts of his 'words', and of the action, 'he saw concerning Israel', are characteristic descriptions of prophets (cp. Micah 1:1), as is everything else we find in the book.

Amos' defensive protest to Amaziah the priest: *I was neither a prophet nor a prophet's son* (7: 14), must be taken with a pinch of salt. They mean no more than that he had had no training to be a prophet, nor did this kind of activity run in the family tradition. Indeed Amos is quite unique in Israel – a warning to professional preachers! He had never been to a school for prophets, a theological college. He was a rustic farmer, but he had an unerring conviction of the call and commission of God, and this was all he needed to go and preach, and his preaching sent shock waves through the northern kingdom.

The most important statement about his ministry is found at 3:7-8. Here he presents the personal defence of his activity. It works like this, he says – all the time we are working on the basis of the observation of cause and effect. He gives examples of these in verses 2-6. You hear a lion growling contentedly, and you deduce from this that he has caught a prey; you hear a trap snap and you reckon that a bird has fallen into it. In the same way, this guy comes preaching. This is what you see and hear. Why does

153

he come and preach, especially if he is an unknown farmer? The simple answer is that *The Sovereign LORD has spoken — who can but prophesy?*

Naive it might have seemed, but it is the heart of the whole nature of Old Testament prophecy. The true prophet is a man (in some cases a woman, 2 Kings 22:14) who has been admitted to the secret counsels of the Most High, and he is commissioned to take this counsel and make it known to his compatriots: *The Sovereign LORD does nothing without revealing his plan to his servants the prophets* (v. 7).

Amos' logical conclusion, *The lion has roared — who will not fear? The Sovereign LORD has spoken — who can but prophesy?*, cannot be bettered. His logic is surely the same as Paul's passionate affirmation: *I am compelled to preach. Woe to me if I do not preach the gospel!* (1 Cor. 9:16). Amos, having stood in the secret counsel of the Lord, is impelled into a proclamation of God's plan.

Prophets in the Bible and Beyond

The appearance of men like Amos throughout the Old Testament is quite remarkable. Not that prophets were unknown outside of Israel, indeed they were a widespread reality in those days. They appear in all kind of ways — as counsellors to kings, as revealers of the gods' will in the temples, as travelling seers, as fortune tellers, etc. Schools for the training of prophets were common. The Old Testament recognises these facts. Balaam was so famous that the King of Moab sent for him to come 300 miles and curse the Israelites (Num. 22:4-5). Queen Jezebel of Israel, before Amos' time, had supported 850 prophets of Baal from the royal purse (1 Kings 18:19).

What is remarkable about Amos and the other Old Testament prophets is their moral integrity. Foreign prophets, and the 'false' prophets of Israel, are little more than fortune-tellers, quacks as we might say. When Amaziah told Amos to go back to his own land, and *Earn your bread there and do your prophesying there* (7:12), he was only expressing his assumption that Amos was like all other prophets, in it for what he could get out of it. Like Satan's accusation of Job, *Does Job fear God for nothing?* (Job 1:9), Amaziah could not believe that Amos acted on utterly pure motives. In reality Amos was doing what he accused the leaders of the nation of not doing, *mourn over the ruin of Israel* (6:6).

If moral integrity was in itself remarkable, what is even more outstanding is the fact that these men were not the products of a naturally good society. There is a notion abroad that Israel was a godly society. Some would say that just as the Greeks gave us philosophy, and the Romans gave us law, so then the genius of the Jewish nation was to give us religion.

What the prophets themselves show us is that far from having a genius for pure religion, the mass of the people and their leaders had a genius for apostasy, expressed in false religion, idolatry, gross immorality and exploitation of the weak and poor. The prophets were not the products of a national religious genius. They are inexplicable, except as evidences of a special working of the Spirit of God to produce men who stood against their own nation. They were swimming against the tide. The cards were stacked against them. They lived dangerously against the mass of popular opinion, much as Christians are called to do today. That is why most moderns are uncomfortable with the prophets of Israel.

The Primary Objectives of Prophecy

Unfortunately in our times there has developed a gross misunderstanding about the nature and objectives of Old Testament prophecy. Popular ideas are well represented in the definition of prophecy found in the *Oxford Dictionary*: 'foretell future events'.

Now our word 'prophecy' is made up of two Greek words, the little word *pro* and the action word *phemi*. The action word means 'to speak', whilst *pro* means 'before', so that prophecy means to 'speak before'. However, *pro* is, like all prepositions, a slippery customer, and will have numerous possible translations into English. The most common would be to say that it means 'for'. A good dictionary will give you ten or more basic meanings, each of which has shades of meaning. Obviously we are not going to get far by analysing words.

The only reasonable way is to look at how prophets and prophecy functioned in Israel. Here a classic passage, outside the prophetical books, is 2 Kings 17, which contains a long explanation as to why Israel was expelled from the land and sent into exile. The foremost reason is this:

> The LORD warned Israel and Judah through all his prophets and seers: 'Turn from your evil ways. Observe my commands and decrees, in accordance with the entire Law that I commanded your fathers to obey and that I delivered to you through my servants the prophets' (v. 13).

The prophets have been called 'covenant enforcement officers'. As we have seen in the chapter on Israel's history, the Lord had given the people his Law, which they had solemnly agreed to keep: 'When Moses ... told the people all the LORD's words and laws, they responded with one voice, "Everything the LORD has said we will do" ' (Exod. 24:3).

A century after Amos, Jeremiah testified: 'The LORD said to me, "Proclaim all these words in the towns of Judah and in the streets of Jerusalem: Listen to the terms of this covenant and follow them" ' (Jer. 11:6). This was the essential function of the prophets. They were not innovators, but simply men who loved God's law, who saw their compatriots turning to evil, and burned with a desire to turn them back to the Lord.

This zeal they saw, not as the natural product of their own heart probing, but of the sure conviction that the Lord had called them to this high duty. It is probable that Amos travelled to the northern kingdom on business, selling his wool and figs, that he saw the idolatry, immorality and injustices which prevailed there, and that his heart burned within him. But he would not have dared confront the priest of Bethel unless convinced that the Lord had called him to do something about it.

It has sometimes been asked whether the prophets were radicals or conservatives. Each political camp would like to take them over. The answer must be that they were radical conservatives. They returned to the old roots of the nation, based on the covenant relationship with Yahweh, spelt out in terms of spiritual, ethical and social requirements, and called the people to return to these in a new and radical way.

The Dangers of the Prophetical Career

Being a true prophet turned out to be a dangerous occupation. We see this in Amos 7 – his confrontation with Amaziah, the priest of Bethel. Finding this mad man (and the prophets were sometimes called mad men, 2 Kings 9:11) preaching in front of the temple at Bethel, Amaziah requested the king to send the necessary powers to have him removed. He even got into a heated public argument with Amos himself, in which Amos seems to have scored a notable success by his courage and boldness.

Various tactics were used to silence these uncomfortable men.

Persuasion. Isaiah testifies to this: 'They [the people] say to the seers, "See no more visions!" and to the prophets, "Give us no more visions of what is right! Tell us pleasant things, prophesy illusions. Leave this way, get off this path, and stop confronting us with the Holy One of Israel" ' (30:10-11). Clearly they found the message of the prophets distinctly uncomfortable and brought pressure to bear on them to change their tune. Some yielded and sold out their vocation: 'If a liar and deceiver comes and says, "I will prophesy for you plenty of wine and beer," he would be just the prophet for this people' (Micah 2:11).

Prohibition. This is the case of priest Amaziah's attack on Amos. He is surely echoing his own experience when he says, 'You ... commanded the prophets not to prophesy' (Amos 2:12, RSV).

Corruption. If threats achieved nothing, the prophet's own conscience could be sullied by corrupting it: 'Priest and prophet stagger from beer and are befuddled with wine; they reel from beer, they stagger when seeing visions, they stumble when rendering decisions' (Isa. 28:7). Once the prophet had been tempted into evil he would be forced to modify his message and thus become a 'false' prophet.

Intimidation, Violence and Death. Prophets who resisted the attempts to silence them faced the possibility of physical intimidation. Micaiah was publicly struck in the face and thrown into prison (1 Kings 22:5-28). Even a relatively godly king like Asa would attempt to silence the prophets if they clashed with his will. After Hanani had rebuked him for seeking help from the Syrians, Asa 'was so enraged that he put him in prison' (2 Chron. 16:10), though it appears that many people supported the prophet, and the king in reaction brutally suppressed all contrary opinion.

It was Jeremiah who most graphically portrayed this intimidation. It seemed that all the world was against him: 'Alas, my mother, that you gave me birth, a man with whom the whole land strives and contends! I have neither lent nor borrowed, yet everyone curses me' (Jer. 15:10).

The opposition quickly degenerated into violence. Jeremiah was born and brought up in the priestly town of Anathoth, four miles from Jerusalem. The people of this town were embarrassed by one of their own preaching against the authorities up in the capital. They tried to silence him: 'Do not prophesy in the name of the LORD or you will die by our hands,' and when the threats achieved nothing, they made a plot to kill him, but fortunately he got wind of it (Jer. 11:18-23). He felt this very keenly. The men with whom he had played in the streets of Anathoth as a boy were now outlawing him.

Worse was to come. Within the year the chief officer of the temple had him whipped and put in the stocks for 24 hours (Jer. 20:1-2). This public humiliation caused him great distress. Shortly after this he was arrested and put on trial for treason (Jer. 26). The chief instigators of this trial were the temple priests and the false prophets. So far from being silenced, Jeremiah used the occasion to preach yet another sermon, warning of the dire consequences of unrepentance. It was only the intervention of the elders, the old clan leaders, and a friend at court, which saved Jeremiah's life.

The same chapter, however, tells of a prophet who was not so fortunate, Uriah by name, against whom the king issued a warrant for his arrest and execution. Uriah fled to Egypt, but King Jehoiakim had him extradited and his head severed publicly with a sword.

Jeremiah felt these events sorely. Indeed he seems to have suffered shock: 'Oh, my anguish, my anguish! I writhe in pain. Oh, the agony of my heart! My heart pounds within me. I cannot keep silent' (Jer. 4.19).

The False Prophets

It is a salutary thought that some of these 'false' prophets were almost certainly originally true prophets. Enormous pressure brought to bear against them forced them into compromise, from which there would be little chance of a return to the initial enthusiasm and purity of intention. Adapting themselves to the ethos of their culture, they no longer stood over against it, but succumbed to it. This meant that when they did prophesy they would say nice things that would play to their hearers' desires. Paul suggests a very similar set of circumstances when he says: 'The time will come when men will not put up with sound doctrine. Instead, to suit their own desires, they will gather around them a great number of teachers to say what their itching ears want to hear' (2 Tim. 4:3).

There was an inherent danger in the office of a prophet. They could become influential and powerful people. In Israel, as in other countries, they could become counsellors of kings. Some could use this for good ends, as in the case of Nathan who condemned David's adultery to his face (2 Sam. 12). Since such counsellors would be paid from the royal purse, their situation could become financially precarious if their royal masters were not disposed to listen to them.

They could become politically involved, as when Solomon secured his throne by obtaining the backing of Zadok the priest, army general Benaiah, alongside that of Nathan the prophet. The latter's influence was as important as that of the 'archbishop' and of the general. Prophetical power was to back-fire for Solomon, for at the end of his reign Ahijah the prophet, scandalised by his idolatry, inspired a movement of opposition (1 Kings 1 and 11).

False prophets became a thorn in the flesh for the true prophets. No prophet was more concerned about them than Jeremiah. In the most important biblical passage on the subject, Jeremiah 23, he accuses them of

- Abusing their power (v. 10)
- Leading godless lives in collusion with evil priests (v. 11)
- Encouraging the people in idolatry (v. 13)
- Committing adultery (v. 14)
- Being in league with those who practised evil (v. 14)
- Of lacking divine call and inspiration

This latter accusation is the heart of his charge. As we saw in Amos, the true prophet stands in the council of the Lord and receives his 'plan' or 'council'. Jeremiah says that this is precisely what the false prophets have not done:

> They speak visions from their own minds,
>   not from the mouth of the LORD ....
> But which of them has stood in the *council* of the LORD
>   to see or to hear his word?....
> I did not send these prophets,
>   yet they have run with their message;
> I did not speak to them,
>   yet they have prophesied.
> But if they had stood in my *council*,
>   they would have proclaimed my words to my people
> and would have turned them from their evil ways
>   and from their evil deeds (Jer. 23:16-22).

He accuses them of prophesying delusions originating in their own minds. Their appeal to dreams he scornfully rejects as vastly inferior to the word of God, as straw is to grain.

The Time-Line of the Prophets of Israel

It is helpful to note the times in which the prophets appeared in Israel. Each important event in her history was accompanied by a prophetic manifestation.

CENTURY BC	PROPHETS	EVENTS
XIII	Moses	The Exodus
X	Samuel, Nathan, Gad, Ahijah	Early Monarchy
IX	Elijah, Elisha, Jonah	Ahab and Baalism
VIII	GOLDEN AGE Amos, Hosea, Isaiah, Micah	Assyrian Empire Fall of Samaria
VII-VI	EXILIC PROPHETS Habakkuk, Nahum, Zephaniah, Obadiah, Jeremiah, Ezekiel, Daniel	Babylonian Empire Fall of Jerusalem
V	POST-EXILIC PROPHETS Haggai, Zechariah, Malachi	Return from Exile

Interpreting the Prophets

We have already seen that there is a tendency to look on the Old Testament prophets as foretellers of the future. Not so. They were primarily seeking to call their own people back to the past, rather than to the future. They wanted the old rules of justice, faithfulness, love and peace to be returned to as the condition for the blessing of the Lord upon the nation.

Let the reader run through the book of Amos and ask himself how much of the prophecy can be called futuristic, i.e. relating to the end times? I think you will find that there is little that can be said to relate in any sense to the future – say 10%? Even then, one has to distinguish between immediate, proximate and end-time prophecy. I suspect that the only passage in Amos which can truly be defined as in some way relating to the end-times is the last one in the book, 9:11-15, where Amos dreams of the future glory of Israel.

Immediate and Proximate Prophecy

In his initial prophecy Amos slams the nations located around Israel and Judah, and assures each one that God is about to bring destruction on their cities. There can be little doubt that Amos expected this to happen fairly soon.

This is also true of his threat of coming disaster to Israel: *Now then, I will crush you as a cart crushes when loaded with grain...* (2:13-16). Indeed the whole 11 chapters centre around the expected coming destruction of Israel: *You only have I chosen of all the families of the earth; therefore I will punish you for all your sins* (3:2); *An enemy will overrun the land; he will pull down your strongholds and plunder your fortresses* (3:11), and very many others.

This is not prophecy directed to the end times. Rather it is on the horizon, soon to break on the nation. It is interesting to note that the prophet nowhere specifies the nation which will destroy Israel, though he is sure there will be one. This is in agreement with the date 760 BC for the book, since Assyria did not begin to move as an empire until the accession of Tiglath-Pileser III in 745. Yet Amos was conscious of the threat which existed from the north, since in 5:27 he predicts an exile beyond Damascus. The great city of Samaria, superbly defended by the walls and gate of kings Omri and Ahab would be destroyed (6:8), and the mansions of the rich would be utterly devastated (6:11). Three of Amos' visions in chapters 7-9 ring with the certainty of the coming destruction.

A word needs to be said here about the particular threat made to Amaziah in 7:17. The latter had called in the authorities to get rid of Amos, and then became involved in a public confrontation. Amos got the last word by declaring that, *Your wife will become a prostitute in the city, and your sons and daughters will fall by the sword. Your land will be measured and divided up, and you yourself will die in a pagan country.* To put it mildly, this sounds vindictive, spiteful, and I suspect that the average modern congregation squirms when it is read in public. But it should be read in the light of the social context and the Lord's message through Amos.

Amaziah, as priest of Bethel, the king's royal chapel, is part and parcel of the evil which is rampant in the land. Instead of standing for the purity of worship he has permitted idolatry; gross immorality after the Canaanite style is happening in his temple; whilst he will have shared in the drunken feasts of the rich made possible through exploitation of the poor. It was not personal insult which angered Amos, but Amaziah's position and his refusal to contemplate repentance and a return to the Lord's ways.

What is more, the prophecy against Amaziah introduces us to a factor about prophecy which is important to notice. The words are not to be taken at face value, much less in the sense that a modern person might read them. They simply describe the natural consequences of ancient warfare. Amos knows that war is coming, that Israel will be ignominiously defeated, and will go into exile far away. On such occasions the men were taken away into exile, whilst all but the most important or beautiful women were left in poverty and misery. Isaiah has a similar picture where the male population has been almost totally annihilated, so that 'seven women will take hold of one man and say, "We will eat our own food and provide our own clothes; only let us be called by your name..." ' (Isa. 4:1).

We shall never know whether Amaziah's wife became a prostitute, nor whether his sons and daughters were killed. Nor indeed does it matter. So long as the main thrust happens, i.e. the defeat of Israel and her exile, the details are simply the furniture of the scene, part of the scenario of ancient warfare, the details are of little importance. This opens us up to the question of how we should interpret biblical prophecy.

How to handle prophecy

It must be understood that biblical prophecy is unlike anything we find in our modern literature. It is characterised by

Conditionality. Much biblical prophecy, though by no means all, is conditional. Jeremiah had himself to learn this lesson, when the Lord told him to go to the house of the potter and watch him at his wheel (Jer. 18). As he watched he saw the potter remaking a pot because it would not yield to the original design. From this he was required to make a comparison with God's way of working in prophecy: 'If at any time I announce that a nation or kingdom is to be uprooted, torn down and destroyed, and if that nation I warned repents of its evil, then I will relent and not inflict on it the disaster I had planned' (Jer. 18:7, 8). God then goes on to say the reverse is also true when he has announced good for a nation and they then do evil. That is, when God intends to do something, and the conditions change, his plan will also change, though guided by infallible truth and righteousness.

We see this idea clearly displayed in the work of Jonah in Nineveh. He prophesied, '40 more days and Nineveh will be overturned' (Jonah 3:4). No 'ifs' or 'buts', you notice, no conditional clauses, no 'unless...'. Nineveh repented, and God turned from his design to destroy the city and saved it. This was a simple outworking of the principle explained to Jeremiah, and was meant to be understood as undergirding prophecy, the conditional element.

Repetitive Character. There is a tendency among many Christians to interpret prophecy as a kind of mathematical equation. 'This is that' is worked out like a neat equation. This that I find in one Scripture, usually the Old Testament, corresponds to that which I encounter in another, often the New Testament. It fits perfectly!

I want to suggest that it is more dynamic than that, and we can do no better than start in the book of Amos to demonstrate this. In chapter 5:18, after berating the Israelites for their perversion of justice, he turns on the religious people:

> *Woe to you who long*
> *for the day of the LORD!*
> *Why do you long for the day of the LORD?*
> *That day will be darkness, not light ....*
> *Will not the day of the LORD be darkness, not light –*
> *pitch-dark, without a ray of brightness?*

Four times he refers to 'the day'. The expression, 'the Day of the Lord' is very common in the Old Testament, but it is never explained. Clearly Amos' hearers understood perfectly what he was saying, and it needed no explanation. It was a popular expression. People were 'longing' for that Day. They evidently anticipated that it would be a good time for them, but not for their enemies. They were sure that their interests were also the interests of God. Amos is seeking to disillusion them. So far from being a happy day, it's going to be very grim indeed. He is convinced that the Day of the Lord will not merely be a time of punishment for

Israel's enemies, but for all evil people, including, and very especially, those of Israel herself.

The moment we compare this with other passages where the expression is used, it is evident that it is a dynamic concept, the day of Yahweh's intervention to punish evil. Most forceful in use of the term is Zephaniah's preaching:

> Listen! The cry on the Day of the LORD will be bitter,
>> the shouting of the warrior there.
> That day will be a day of wrath,
>> a day of distress and anguish,
> a day of trouble and ruin,
>> a day of darkness and gloom,
>> a day of clouds and blackness,
> a day of trumpet and battle cry ....
> I will bring distress on the people [of Israel]
>> (Zeph. 1:14-17, see also 2:1-2).

He terms it 'the Day of the Lord's wrath'. It is probable that his preaching moved the heart of the young king Josiah to introduce far-reaching religious reforms.

Some other occasions in which the term is used:

1. The Day of the LORD is a plague of locusts (Joel 1:15; 2:1-11). In a vision Joel sees a plague of locusts devastating the land. In this case the Day of the LORD is even now present, and Joel knows that only repentance can save the nation. Yet it is important to notice that later Joel sees this plague of locusts as a portent of future and final events (Joel 2:31; 3:14).

2. Isaiah, citizen of Jerusalem, sees the Day of the LORD hovering over that city in judgment, whilst for the writer of Lamentations it had become a reality as he wandered in agony among the ruins of that city more than 100 years later (Isa. 2:12; Lam. 1:12; 2:1-2).

3. Isaiah, looking into the future, used the language of the Day of the LORD to describe the day in which Babylon would fall to the Medes (13:6,9 with 17-19). It happened 200 years later in 539 BC.

From these examples we can see the fluid nature of the Day of the Lord. It is not a static concept, but a dynamic one. Why does Joel see the Day of the Lord as a plague of locusts? Because from his standpoint any divine intervention may be the last one. And even if it wasn't, it could be seen as shadow and foretaste of the final disaster. Once we grasp this we shall see that it is dangerous to be dogmatic about the exact interpretation of particular prophecies.

The 'Shadow' Character of Old Testament Prophecy. The apostle Paul made a key interpretative statement about the Old Testament in Colossians 2:17: 'These are a shadow of the things that were to come; the reality, however, is found in Christ.' The word translated 'reality' is literally 'body (*soma*)'. The human body throws a shadow. If I see my wife's shadow I would probably recognise it immediately and would be able to say a lot about her. If, however, I were to see the shadow of a person unknown to me, it would tell me very little about the person. I might form an idea, but on meeting the person I would almost certainly realise how very poor my guess work was.

What I mean is that it is the body which is the reality, and the shadow can only hint at some elements of the body. So it is with the Old and New Testaments. The Old Testament, the shadow, has hints of greater things to come. It has hopes and aspirations which are often frustrated. It raises questions and mysteries for which it cannot suggest a satisfying answer. Yet it prepares for the coming of the 'body', the reality, the decisive revelation of God in Jesus the Messiah.

It follows that if the Old Testament persons, events, and institutions are only 'shadows', then they must always be interpreted and re-interpreted, in the light of the New. They have no meaning to which the New Testament must rigidly conform. They are dynamic, fluid, flexible, and only the New Testament can give Old Testament prophecy its definitive meaning.

The Poetic Character of Prophecy. It is an unfortunate fact that for 300 years English-speaking Christians read prophecy in the Authorised Version, which reproduced it in prose form. Prose is generally used for making statements of fact, whereas poetry is designed to produce a feeling, an emotion, an ethos, a reaction. The last thing poetry is intended for is making statements of facts. Poetry uses vivid imagery to drive its point home. Much of this imagery is simply the scenery behind the central intention. To seek to find some form of fulfilment behind this imagery is to rob the poetry of its force.

Fantasy is a legitimate usage of poetry. Isaiah 34:8-15 taken literally would present animals and birds walking and nesting on burning pitch! In reality we have two sets of metaphors placed side-by-side. May there not be an element of fantasy in all futuristic prophecy, incapable of explanation, rational or otherwise? It is not meant to be explained, it is meant to be felt, as Marc Chagall said of one of his paintings. It is difficult for the Western mind to understand the primacy of the imagination over reason. In the East vivid imagination was and still is the norm, and this is typical of the biblical way of speaking.

The Dream-like Character of Prophecy. The two words 'vision' and 'dream' seem to be interchangeable in the Old Testament. Jeremiah brings this out in his 31st chapter. For two chapters he has waxed enthusiastic about the promised return of the Israelites to their land after the exile. Signposts are dotted along the way, the crowds stream back, the Gentiles help them on their way, and Jerusalem is wonderfully restored to its former glory. Then suddenly he says, 'At this I awoke and looked around. My sleep had been pleasant to me' (31:26). Indeed it had! Now the very nature of dreams is that they are fuzzy at the edges. The central realities express our hopes, aspirations and fears, but there is a lot mixed in there which is totally confusing, even meaningless. May not prophecy, which is often received in visions and dreams, be similar? Incidentally, neither at the beginning, nor at the end, does Jeremiah indicate that this was a vision/dream.

The Central Prophetic Passage of Amos

Amos 9:11-15 should be read at this point. Most of his prophecies relate to the immediate future, in particular to the coming destruction and exile of the northern kingdom. This passage projects us beyond that to some glorious day when Israel will be restored, her cities rebuilt, and her protection for ever guaranteed. In exuberant language those days are described as the time *when corn will grow faster than it can be harvested, and grapes will grow faster than the wine can be made. The mountains will drip with sweet wine, and the hills will flow with it* (verse 13, GNB). A graphic picture of the super-abundance which will characterise Israel's future.

One could hardly believe that Amos intended these words were meant to be taken literally. They are simply meant to convey a sense of the abundant provisions which God will make for his people.

Amos is a figure of Christ!

This may seem a rather unusual thing to say, yet it holds a large amount of truth. In a sense all God's servants point us to Christ Jesus. That is true even today. What I see of goodness and truth in the life of any child or servant of God points me to Christ, and if that is so outside divine revelation, how much more within it. Amos' rugged defence of the truth of God's law, his opposition to all hypocrisy, the purity of the truth he preached, his willingness to endanger his own life over against the representatives of political power, all point us to Christ, who did all this to perfection.

Yet this 'figure' of Christ is an imperfect shadow. It seems, I think, to the normal reader that Amos' emphasis on divine judgment is stronger than any other prophet, and is seldom balanced by stressing also his grace and forgiveness, though these are there if you scratch the surface. But this is true in some way or other of every Old Testament figure, as well as its events and institutions.

Moses seems a perfect salvation figure, leading the people from the slavery of Egypt into the glorious liberty of the children of God, yet his breaking of the commandment tablets brought God's condemnation. David was a figure of kingship which lived long in the memories of the Israelites, but his adultery with Bathsheba and its consequences stained his record. Some thought that when Jesus appeared he was a new appearance of Jeremiah, yet the latter's inability to understand the meaning of his own suffering stands in bold contrast to Jesus' perfect comprehension of the will of his Father. By the very nature of things all those things which in the Old Testament seem to point us to Christ are shadowy figures, which direct us only obliquely to Jesus.

Messianic Prophecy

There is a line of Old Testament prophecy which is clearly intended to point to the future, and which is clear as to its meaning, free of ambiguity. Fulfilment is the vindication of the prophet (Deut. 18:21-22), yet it is not the conclusive vindication, for even a false prophet might see remarkable fulfilments of his prophecies (Deut. 13:1-3). What is more, the true prophets often had to wait a long time before fulfilment happened. This then led to some heart-searching on their part, and ridicule from their ungodly hearers.

The most striking and clear statements of future prophecy relate to the coming of Messiah (Christ). Isaiah is the most powerful in this sense. His promise of the coming of a child is well-known to most readers through the Christmas reading:

For to us a child is born,
    to us a son is given,
    and the government will be on his shoulders.
And he will be called
    Wonderful Counsellor, Mighty God,
    Everlasting Father, Prince of Peace.
Of the increase of his government and peace
    there will be no end.
He will reign on David's throne
    and over his kingdom,
establishing and upholding it
    with justice and righteousness
    from that time on and for ever (Isa. 9:6-7).

What we do not always appreciate about these powerful words is that they were born out of national disaster. In 732 BC Tiglath-Pileser III of Assyria had invaded the northern kingdom and carried away the inhabitants of Galilee into far away lands. Isaiah feels the anguish of this loss of his fellow countrymen, for though the split of the north from the south was an established fact, the prophets still regarded the two nations as one people. Verse 1 of the chapter paints the deep gloom into which Galilee had been plunged, but looks to a day when the gloom will be lifted, when the 'enlarged nation' (v. 3) will experience peace along with all mankind (v. 5), which can only happen when the 'child is born' (v. 6).

Matthew, in his Gospel, does not hesitate to apply the prophecy of the scattering of Galilee's gloom to the public ministry of Jesus in that area (Matt. 4:15-16), and this leads us back to the important principle of the multiple levels of fulfilment of a prophecy, or its repetitive nature.

These repetitions are due to the very nature of God. Because the Old Testament picture of God is that he is utterly consistent in all that he does, the acts of God are repeated in history. The prophet however, sees these from a foreshortened perspective. Things are 'telescoped', so as to form one panorama, like superimposed pictures. Thus in Isaiah 52:4-10, we find the Egyptian bondage and the Assyrian oppression (v. 4); the Babylonian exile (v. 5); gospel salvation (v. 7); and expectation of the end times (vv. 8-10), all fused into one. The present, the past and the future, the declaratory and the predictive are all combined and fused. It is disastrous to read prophecy on a unifocal time frame. It would seem better to suggest that the prophets themselves were conscious of working on a multiple time frame.

Ezekiel, toward the end of the Old Testament era, introduces the curious evil figure of Gog: 'Are you not the one I spoke of in former days by my servants the prophets of Israel? At that time they prophesied for years that I would bring you against them' (Ezek. 38:17). Now you will look in vain for any prophet prior to Ezekiel who ever spoke of an evil figure called Gog. What they do have in common with Ezekiel's Gog is that they saw a threat to Israel emanating from the north, sometimes in the Assyrians, other times the Babylonians. So Ezekiel must mean that the evil manifest in Assyria and Babylonia is the same which will at the end times be seen in Gog. The same spirit infuses them all.

This leads me to suggest the following scheme:

The Prophet	»	Immediate Event	»	The Christ Event	»	End Time Event

The immediate, national event is the Type, of which both the Christ Event and the End Time Event are the Antitype.

Scholars usually refer to the Christ Event as the Christological Event, and the End Time Event as the Eschatological. It is important to note here that what the prophet sees is the immediate event, though often with shades of the Christ and End Time events included. We might compare it with a bowman looking at a small target, behind which stand two larger targets, partially eclipsed by the first, small target. The historical, the Christological and the eschatological here are blurred together in his eyes.

Applying the principle of multiple fulfilment we can return to the figure of Gog. The New Testament use of the figure portrayed in Ezekiel 38 and 39 is instructive. Revelation 20:7 says: 'And when the thousand years are ended, Satan will be loosed from his prison and will come out to deceive the nations which are at the four corners of the earth, that is, Gog and Magog to gather them for battle.' So we can say that the writer sees the appearance of this sinister figure, of Satanic origin, *after* the thousand years, whatever we may take these years to mean.

However, if we turn to Revelation 19:17-18 we find that the author uses the language of Ezekiel 39:17-20 to provide the details for a great battle which is to take place *before* the 1000 years, and that he also uses Ezekiel 38 and 39 in Revelation 16:18-20 to describe earlier skirmishes in the final battles of evil against God's throne. John does not limit the fulfilment of prophecy to one event. This must be because he believed that wherever the spirit of evil is manifest, there the spirit of Gog, of Satan, of the Antichrist, clashes with the kingdom of God. So, whether Ezekiel is looking backward, or the New Testament is looking ahead, the prophecy is considered fluid, dynamic.

Gog, we might say, is a personification of evil in time and space (history and geography). He is at the same time a *forecast*, a *foretelling*, and a *foretaste* of the ultimate manifestation of evil.

It is not really then a question of the New Testament *interpretation* of the Old Testament prophecy, but of its *application*. The New Testament does not so much interpret the Old Testament, as apply it to the new situation in which the writer/speaker finds himself. He works in a radically different situation, brought about by the coming of Christ. He uses the Old Testament material creatively in the light of the new reality. I have no doubt that it was Jesus himself who taught the disciples to do this. In this application of the Old Testament the New Testament writers exercise a freedom under the Spirit, though they usually show they are not ignorant of the Old Testament context and intent.

Christ Jesus – the Key to all Prophecy

But what of divine intention? We may discern a certain flexibility in the application of the Old Testament prophecy, but can we discern what God intended? The first obvious reply is that God intended this very flexibility. The literalist approach displays a legalistic mind. The Jews felt they could be acceptable to God if they tithed, even to the smallest garden herb, but found justice, kindness and faithfulness much too rigorous a demand (Matt. 23:23).

In the same way it is too easy to see the New Testament fulfilment as a straight line, going straight to a literal target. The situation is more dynamic, rather like a zig-zag line, and a line which might hit at various points.

There is one saving feature to all this. It is that Jesus Christ is the heart and centre of all Old Testament prophecy, and, indeed, of every other hope and aspiration. He accused the Jewish leaders: 'You diligently study the Scriptures because you think that by them you possess eternal life' (John 5:39). They were barking up the wrong tree. Scripture is never an end in itself, but a means to an end. So he goes on to say in the same verse: 'These are the Scriptures that testify about me ....'

Amos and his book are not an end in themselves. They are not given to us as historical curiosities, nor yet that we might become diligent interpreters of its meaning, and even the meaning of the whole Old Testament. Rather the book is designed to point beyond itself. Pointing to the disaster of the people of God, it hints at, and sometimes positively affirms greater things to come.

So when the early Christians wanted to interpret and justify their acceptance of non-Jews into the early church, they did so by appealing to Amos 9:11-12 (see Acts 15:16-17). Amos had hinted at a salvation which would be greater than the narrow confines of Israel, since it would include *all the nations that bear my name.*

They saw that with the coming of Christ Amos' vision had reached fulfilment, or perhaps better fill-full-ment!

In Christ Jesus all the hopes, dreams, and aspirations of the people of God, of prophets, priests and wise men, have come to their fill-full-ment.

Conclusion

Let us pick up the threads. We have used the book of Amos as a launching pad to encourage us to get into the message of the Old Testament as a whole. We saw the need for a hands-on approach, and this has led us through the various disciplines which are necessary to understand the biblical text.

I want to reiterate what I said in the Introduction. It is not necessary to know and master these disciplines in order to understand the spiritual message. Amos' confrontation with Amaziah at Bethel carries its own message, as the time-serving priest tries to silence the itinerant prophet. It is a message of enormous courage on Amos' part, of purity of intention, of dedication to service, of placing one's life on the line in order to do God's will. Amaziah becomes a warning to us all of the grave dangers to those who hold power, that power leads to social, moral and spiritual corruption. The coercion he uses to get rid of Amos was an abuse of power. He required a pack of lies in order to back it up.

All of this lies on the surface, but beneath the surface, with the use of the various disciplines, we have found much that will enrich our lives, our thinking, and our ministry.

I once heard Alec Motyer say that we should be about the business of getting Christians into the Old Testament and the Old Testament into Christians. How exciting. The Old Testament is about 2/3 of the Bible, the Word of God. Truly a new Christian should start his spiritual pilgrimage in the New Testament, but he will soon find that this urgently needs to be complemented with the Old. In a sense the New presumes that you have done your homework in the Old.

We have seen that the geography of the land of Israel gives us the spacial context in which the history of the people is worked out. History, geography and culture add many graphic details to our understanding, our mental reconstruction, of what happened. This history is not a bare facts history. The biblical historian interprets the facts, showing us the moral and spiritual decisions which its heroes and villains make on their journey through life. To join its heroes is to identify ourselves with their struggles and insights. Our theology, like that of the heroes, is worked out at the coal-face of life, as we stand alongside them.

Behind Amos' denunciation of evil lies a strong theology. Theology is simply the way of thinking about God. We are all engaged in it, in some form or other. By nature we are as blind as bats. The God of Israel is the creator of heaven and earth, who loves goodness and hates evil. When evil grows and prevails he moves into action to destroy it. Yet basically he yearns for his people, and longs to see them turn from wrong to seek the good life.

There are two sources of Amos' theological thought. In the first place Amos is the inheritor of a tradition passed down through his people, a tradition which goes back to Abraham and Moses. He is a messenger of the covenant, which the Lord had established through Moses hundreds of years before. The other source of his theology is his certainty that God in his wisdom speaks to his servants the prophets, whom he admits to his counsel and sends to their fellow men to turn them from evil.

This theology is worked out within the limits of the literary forms of his contemporaries. God does not use Amos like a typist uses a Personal Computer. He had made Amos the man he wanted him to be, forming his character amidst the harsh realities of Tekoa on the edge of the Judean desert. His teaching uses the natural vessels of communication – human language, with all its frailty and limitations.

We looked at the social structures of Amos' days, and saw they are not unlike those which we find in our own societies. The abuse of power and the exploitation of our fellows is as real today as it was when Amos so fiercely denounced it in Israel. We have not learnt much, and the further our society moves away from the biblical message, so much the more will idolatry (sports, music, media and entertainment idols, etc.), immorality (sexual indulgence, pornography, rape, child sexual abuse, divorce, etc.) and injustice (laws loaded to favour the rich) prevail among us.

Finally we turned to prophecy. We saw the prophet as God's messenger, a quite unique event on the human scene. Not that there were not prophets in other nations, but these tended to be little more than fortune tellers, whereas the Hebrew prophets, like Amos, stood apart from their generation. They were not there to entertain, to smooth over life's difficulties, to make people feel comfortable with whatever lifestyle they chose. They came to call them back to the ways of the Lord. They were sent to enforce God's moral law.

At the same time the prophets were not merely preachers for their generation, they also contained an amount of future visions. We have seen that at every level the Old Testament reaches a point beyond which it is unable to go, and that it points beyond itself to those superb uses of it in the New Testament. The Old Testament may truly be said to be centred on Christ, i.e. Christocentric, for he becomes the answer to its queries and intentions, its anticipations, hopes and dreams.

I trust I have gone some way to responding to latent questions in your mind, that I have whetted your tongue to an appetite for more of these two-thirds of the Word of God.

Appendix

Archaeology and the Book of Amos

Archaeology related to the Bible is an enormous subject. It has thrown a very great light upon many obscure references and has authenticated many biblical events. For our purposes we shall only consider a few findings which illuminate our understanding of the book of Amos.

We might discourse here on possible archaeological remains at Tekoa and Bethel, and many other places mentioned, but it seems more profitable and interesting to mention a few discoveries which illuminate the text of Amos.

Numerical sayings

For three sins of Damascus, even for four..., (1:3 and six times thereafter). We have already noted the connection between these and similar numeric sayings in the Wisdom books. Even more interesting is that we find this form also used in Canaanite works more than 700 years before Amos in archaeological remains located hundreds of miles north of Palestine.

Consider the following:

> For two kinds of banquets Baal hates,
> Three the Rider of the clouds:
> A banquet of shamefulness,
>   a banquet of baseness,
>   and a banquet of handmaids' lewdness.[1]

Similarly from the same source:

> Three months it is that he has been ill,
> Four that Keret has been sick

---

[1]Translation by H. L. Ginsburg, *Ancient Near Eastern Texts*, Princeton University Press, 1969, p. 147.

and from Assyria we find a similar one:

> Two things are meet, and the third pleasing to Shamash:
>> one who drinks wine and gives to drink,
>> one who guards wisdom, and
>> one who hears a word and does not tell.

Once again we see the way in which the biblical writers moved in a sphere of discourse which was common to people everywhere in the ancient Near East. This way of speaking may sound strange to us, but it was everyday conversation in that time and place.

Taking a man's cloak as a pawn item (2:7f.), is corroborated both by Exodus 22:26f.: 'If you take your neighbour's cloak as a pledge, return it to him by sunset, because the cloak is the only covering he has for his body', and by a find on the coast of Israel. It is in the form of a letter to a city governor, and was found in a storeroom beside the gate of a fortress:

> 'Let my lord commander hear the case of his servant .... your servant was harvesting ....While your servant was finishing the storage of the grain with his harvesters, Hoshaiah son of Shobai came and took your servant's mantle. It was while I was finishing with my harvesters that this one for no reason took your servant's mantle .... All my companions will testify on my behalf. If I am innocent of guilt, let him return my mantle, and if not, it is still the commander's right to take my case under advisement and to send word to him asking that he return the mantle of your servant.'[2]

In this passage it is clear that Hoshaiah was not a common thief. He took the cloak openly and unashamedly, evidently because he was determined to use it as some kind of legal pawn. The writer's appeal is that he is innocent of any charge with which Hoshaiah

---

[2]Translation by W. F. Albright, *Ancient Near Eastern Texts*, Princeton University Press, 1969, p. 568.

will justify his taking the cloak, and his appeal to the city governor is based on his injured sense of justice. It is clearly a very similar case to the act mentioned by Amos.

The 'Shame' of Samaria

An interesting archaeological discovery sheds light on a rather difficult passage of Amos (8:14): *They who swear by the shame of Samaria, or say, 'As surely as your god lives, O Dan', or 'As surely as the god of Beersheba lives'*. Graffiti scratched on rock in northern Sinai reads: 'I bless you by Yahweh of Samaria and by Asherata', and, 'I bless you by Yahweh of Teman and by Asherata'.

Now what these two sentences have in common with the Amos passage is that they clearly indicated that 'gods' were linked to particular places – Samaria and Teman. So in Amos gods are linked to Samaria, Dan and Beersheba. Amos, so far from admitting that what the people of Samaria were worshipping was divinely ordained, calls it satirically 'Shame', i.e. it is idolatry of which they should be ashamed. Something else we learn from the inscriptions is that the worship of Yahweh had become so degenerate that people linked the God of Israel with 'Asherata', goddesses believed to bring fertility through sexual acts.

'House of David' at Dan

Taking a tour party to Israel in 1993, we were rather disappointed that we were refused access to the southern gateway, as archaeologists were digging there. Two remarkable discoveries were made. One was the very large complex of the gateway, probably the largest in biblical Israel. In 1996 we had the pleasure of walking up through the gateway, and it was indeed very impressive. However, the other discovery was even more impressive and important. It was of a stele which records the first reference to David's dynasty outside the Bible, and dated by archaeologists to within 50 years of the break up of Solomon's kingdom.

Many other examples could be given, but these will suffice to show the importance of archaeology both to historic events, and to the general ethos of Amos, and of the whole of the Biblical record.

Scripture references

183

Bible themes

The following Focus on the Bible Old Testament commentaries will be available by December 1997.

Author profiles

Stephen Dray is a lecturer at Moorlands College, Bournemouth, England and is also editor of *Evangel*. He has written several books.

David Searle is the Warden of Rutherford House, Edinburgh, Scotland. He has also written *Be Strong in the Lord*, a study of Ephesians 6.

Richard Pratt is Professor of Old Testament at Reformed Theological Seminary, Orlando, USA and author of several books.

Allan Harman is Professor of Old Testament at Presbyterian Theological College, Melbourne, Australia.

Robert Fyall lectures in Old Testament at St. John's College, Durham, England. He has also written *How God Treats His Friends*, a study of the Book of Job.

Michael Eaton is a pastor in Nairobi, Kenya, with the Chrisco Fellowship of Churches. He has written on several subjects including the Tyndale Old Testament commentary on *Ecclesiastes* and the commenatry on *1, 2, 3 John* in the Focus on the Bible series.

John L. Mackay is Professor of Old Testament in the Free Church College, Edinburgh, Scotland.

Bill Cotton is lecturer in Biblical Studies at Moorlands College, Sopley, Christchurch, England. Prior to his current position, Bill was for twenty years a missionary in Bolivia and Argentina. He regularly leads tours to Israel.